Haunted Places
of
Surrey

John Janaway

COUNTRYSIDE BOOKS
NEWBURY BERKSHIRE

COUNTRYSIDE BOOKS
3 Catherine Road
Newbury, Berkshire

To view our complete range of books,
please visit us at
www.countrysidebooks.co.uk

ISBN 1 85306 932 9
EAN 978 1 85306 932 1

Designed by Peter Davies, Nautilus Design

Produced through MRM Associates Ltd., Reading
Typeset by Techniset Typesetters, Newton-le-Willows
Printed by Woolnough Bookbinding Ltd., Irthlingborough

·Contents·

Haunted Places of Surrey

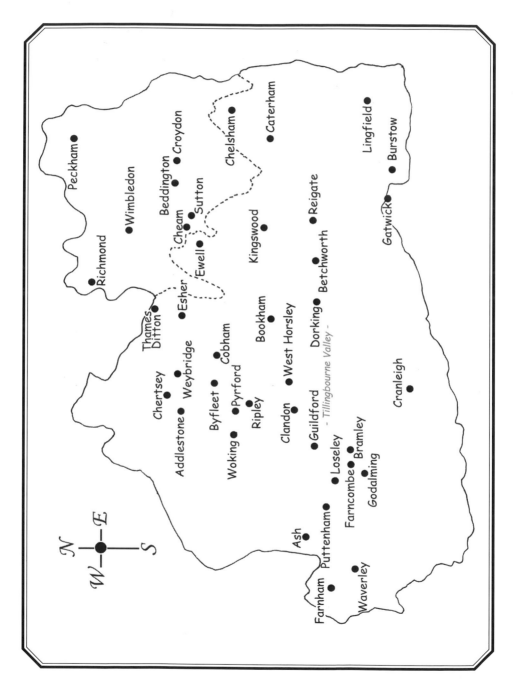

Peckham

Richmond

Wimbledon

Beddington

Croydon

Cheam

Sutton

Ewell

Chelsham

Caterham

Lingfield

Burstow

Kingswood

Reigate

Betchworth

Gatwick

Thames Ditton

Esher

Chertsey

Weybridge

Cobham

Bookham

West Horsley

Dorking

Addlestone

Byfleet

Pyrford

Ripley

Clandon

Guildford

Cranleigh

- Tillingbourne Valley -

Woking

Loseley

Bramley

Farncombe

Godalming

Ash

Puttenham

Farnham

Waverley

N · E · S · W

4

· Introduction ·

For over all there hung a cloud of fear,
A sense of mystery the spirit daunted,
And said, as plain as whispers in the air,
The place is haunted!

Thomas Hood (1799-1845)

I have come to the conclusion that Surrey must be the most haunted county in England. Thomas Hood's description can be applied to numerous places in the area where stories of the strange, macabre and inexplicable abound, so many in fact that this book can only be a selection.

Over many years my research into the county's history has involved the interpretation of facts revealed through old documents and through memories recalled. However, such investigations are really about the lives of those who have peopled the past and, wherever the local historian goes in the present, those people are never far away. Perhaps, they are closer than we think and, as Marconi claimed, they still exist in a parallel world from where occasionally they cross to touch our lives. Whether he was right or not I leave the reader to decide.

John Janaway

ACKNOWLEDGEMENTS

I am very grateful for all the help I have received from so many people during the compilation of this book. I would particularly like to thank Matthew Alexander of Guildford Museum for access to his files of research into Surrey's many ghosts, Brian Boyd for his support and encouragement, and Surrey Archaeological Society and their assistant librarian, Sheila Ashcroft, for help with illustrations. Many thanks also are due to Philip Hutchinson, Sally Jenkinson, Duncan Mirylees, Graham Stevens, the Surrey History Centre at Woking, David Taylor, Andrew Theophanous and above all, to my wife, Sue.

·Surrey·

ADDLESTONE

Those architectural experts Nikolaus Pevsner and Ian Nairn called Addlestone 'a spiritless mixture', a comment which is not entirely true as far as ghosts are concerned. The church of St

School Lane, Addlestone, at the junction with Church Road, where footsteps have been heard late at night. (Author)

Paul is certainly unusual for Surrey, built of stock brick – but they described it as possessing 'a grim, lean exterior'. Nearby, at least one haunting has added just a little spirit to that Addlestone mixture.

One night in October 1953, a local police constable was patrolling his beat along Church Road, when he stopped opposite the junction with School Lane near St Paul's church. It was a very still, quiet evening with no appreciable wind and the streets were completely deserted. Then, in a moment, the peace of the night was disturbed when a strange breeze sprang up, rustling through the branches of the trees in the churchyard across the road. Then came the sound of footsteps, slow and deliberate, walking straight towards him.

Feeling a little unnerved, the policeman shone his torch in the direction of the nocturnal rambler, up the road towards Spinney Hill and the way to Ottershaw. But there was no one there. He crossed the road into School Lane thinking that perhaps the sounds may actually be coming from there. He heard the footsteps quicken, then slow, then stop. The breeze ceased. The streets remained deserted.

Two decades later a cleaner, returning up Church Road after a late shift, also heard those footsteps as they passed the entrance to School Lane and the church. He hurried on a little way before curiosity got the better of him. Stopping momentarily, he turned to look back down the road towards the crossroads. Did he see the wisp of a figure, a woman, grey and transparent? Perhaps not, for the street was empty as before.

ASH

Many are the tales of phantom coaches rumbling through the towns and villages of Surrey, re-enacting some early disaster upon our roads. Maybe in the future there will come tales of spectral 4 x 4s meeting their mangled end in similar circumstances. The coach at Ash is well attested because in 1938 it was seen by the parish rector, the Reverend W J Blaikie, when it disturbed him from his slumbers at Ash Rectory.

'I was awakened by the thud of horses' hooves and the sound of a horn', he reported. 'The coach came in the back way and drove straight through the house and made towards the church.' The rector got a good view of the driver and was able to describe him in some detail. 'He was wearing a scarlet 17th or 18th-century uniform. He seemed quite a cheerful person, and I am under the distinct impression that he turned round as I gazed after him and gave me a cheery salutation with his whip.'

The Reverend Blaikie had come to Ash in 1936 and was soon warned about the phantom coach. 'I was first told about this ghost, which was supposed to haunt the rectory, about a year ago by the wife of a vicar in a neighbouring parish', the rector told a national newspaper. 'The story was that a road used to pass through the site where my predecessors were inconsiderate enough to build the rectory. Afterwards it was said that a phantom coach and four used to ride through the rectory as if it did not exist. On the night when I saw and heard this coach and four, all thoughts of the ghostly visitation had long gone from my mind.'

The rector was very matter-of-fact about what he had seen. 'I have not seen this phantom coach since, but I do not mind if I do. If the rectory must have a ghost, it is as well that it should be a jolly one,' he concluded.

The most famous haunting to be recorded in Ash took place after the Kelly family moved into Ash Manor in 1934.

Late one evening, soon after she came to live at the house, Mrs Kelly was disturbed by a sudden and violent outburst of moans, groans and screams, sounding as if someone was in great pain. Later, the whole family began to hear faltering footsteps along the upstairs corridor. Someone was walking painfully and slowly above their heads, although they knew that there was no one but the family at home. With the footsteps came the terrible noise of suffering and the family began to hear more distressing sounds with increasing frequency as the days went by.

As the months passed into years these eerie noises came more and more often and were ever more unbearable to hear. Desperately the family sought

Does the haunting of Ash Manor indicate a troubled past? (Surrey Archaeological Society)

a solution and, in July 1937, they invited a group of psychic researchers to the house in the hope that they might find a cause. In the party was an American medium, Mrs Garrett, and in a séance she claimed to have made contact with the troubled spirit that stalked the house. The spirit told of family death and imprisonment at the manor, of terrible torture and starvation.

Several séances were held at Ash Manor but eventually the researchers departed, leaving a family hoping that they had rid the unhappy house of its suffering ghost. But that was not to be. The haunting continued until one morning in 1950 when an electricity inspector discovered Mr Kelly lying dead on the front lawn of the manor. Two letters and a bottle of cyanide were beside the body. It could be that the troubled spirit at Ash Manor had taken its revenge but whether this tragic death brought lasting peace to the troubled house we may never know.

BEDDINGTON

Both Beddington and West Horsley lay claim to a ghostly association with that famous character of the late Tudor period, Sir Walter Raleigh. He was a popular man with Queen Elizabeth I until his passionate affair with Elizabeth Throckmorton, one of the queen's ladies-in-waiting, became public knowledge. The Queen was not amused and promptly shoved the loving couple into the Tower of London. Eventually they got out and married but, after Elizabeth's death in 1603 at Richmond, Sir Walter failed miserably to find favour at the court of King James I. Two more visits to the Tower befell the unfortunate man until, in 1618, James had Sir Walter's head chopped off.

Nearly five hundred years on from the moment when Raleigh's head rolled away from his body, there has been much discussion concerning the exact location of his burial. The strongest evidence appears to point to St Margaret's church, Westminster, but the churchyard at Beddington also has a claim. It has been suggested that the body, minus its head, was brought to Beddington, the family home of Raleigh's wife. Lady Raleigh was anxious that her husband's body should rest with those of her family, the Throckmortons and Carews, who were the squires of Beddington. There is no documentary evidence that this actually happened; however, some might say that events over the centuries since have provided sufficient proof to show that this is true. Beddington, and especially the cemetery of its parish church, are haunted and anyone brave enough to walk in the vicinity at night may see the proof. A headless body clad in Tudor clothes wanders here. It could be that it is Sir Nicholas Carew, who also lost his head, but most would claim it for Sir Walter. It searches for its missing head, perhaps, and where that is who can say.

BETCHWORTH

Betchworth is an archetypal English village with its close grouping of cottages, the church of St Michael and the nearby Dolphin pub. Some of the houses have origins in the medieval period and there is even a castle sited some distance from the village centre.

Betchworth Castle received two licences to crenellate, firstly in 1379 and then in 1448. However, it was never intended as a defensive fortress but rather as a smart place in which to live and to show off one's wealth to the neighbours. It was partially demolished in 1690 and then finally dismantled in 1860. The remaining fragments made a fine park folly and, from a distance, they look fairly sinister. Such remains are guaranteed to be the stuff of ghostly legends and Betchworth Castle is no exception.

The place has its own black dog, which lopes around the ruins but answers to the call of nobody and then vanishes. Also a figure of nobility walks the ruins searching for his lost son. The quest is never ending for the son is dead, dead because he was killed accidentally by his own father, a haunting prospect if ever there was one.

One night in the early 1920s, a motorist was driving along the road between Betchworth and Dorking, which in those days was merely a narrow lane. His visibility was dependent on the pale glimmer from a single acetylene lamp mounted on the front offside of his car. At best this enabled him to see no more than a hundred yards ahead. Suddenly the driver was shocked to come upon a large shire horse, complete with harness, galloping head-on at full tilt out of the darkness towards him. He realised instantly that a collision was inevitable as the horse showed no sign of slowing, so he rapidly brought the car to a halt. It only took a second or two but, as so often happens in these situations, time seemed to slow down. Nearer and nearer came the steed, its thick mane and tail flowing in the wind, the motorist gripped by the fear that there was something very strange about this beast. Then, at the moment of impact, it rushed silently by him, passing to his right and almost touching him as it did so. The driver noticed that the previously solid looking animal was now transparent and that he could dimly see the roadside right through its body. He looked behind, back down the road, but the horse had gone on silent hooves. He turned the car round and drove back towards Betchworth hoping that he might discover the answer to the mysterious horse he had clearly seen. But no answer did he find.

Since that time there have been a number of reported sightings of this equine spectre, both in the remaining stretches of the old lane and along the new road to Dorking, but still there is no explanation for the animal's frightening nocturnal gallops.

BOOKHAM

In the ancient parish of Great Bookham is an estate called Slyfield, the origins of which go back to Saxon times. The 'Sly' part of the name is thought to mean 'slippery place', a not too surprising derivation considering its location on the banks of the river Mole. It is from here that an important Surrey family, the Slyfields, acquired their surname. They laid claim to the estate from at least the time when King Richard (the Lionheart) returned to England from the Holy Land in 1194. This king, who has certainly benefited from a history written by his supporters, journeyed back via Cyprus and a Hapsburg castle in central Europe, where he had been imprisoned on his way home. The ransom paid by the good people of England for his safe return nearly bankrupted the country. No doubt the Slyfield family had to chip in. Throughout Richard's entire reign of ten years he deigned to spend a mere six months in England.

A blue donkey has been seen jumping the dog-gate at Slyfield House.
(Surrey Archaeological Society)

The manor house built at Slyfield still retains some timbers which probably date from the time of Nicholas Slyfield, who died in about 1395. However, the building we see today dates from the first part of the 17th century – a fine house, although much was lost when parts of the building were knocked down in the Georgian period. Nearby, the separate Slyfield Farm was once part of a wing of the main house.

Slyfield has staged the usual ups and downs during its centuries of history, including the conviction of Edmund Slyfield for murder. It comes as no surprise to find that some of the cast from this pageant of history still walk its corridors and gardens. For a start, that old friend so popular in Surrey, the blue donkey, has a long tradition of appearances at Slyfield. At the foot of the main Jacobean staircase there is a dog gate. In times past dogs would be released to roam the ground floor at night to deter any intruders and the gate prevented the dogs from straying upstairs. At midnight on certain days of the year, the blue donkey at Slyfield jumps the dog gate, makes its way up the stairs and vanishes on reaching the top.

In the gardens, an unhappy grey lady, her dismal features fixed and staring, listlessly plods her silent progress. But the peace is often broken by the pounding of hooves, the rattle and grind of wheels and shouts of the ostlers as an invisible coach draws into a defunct courtyard.

Inside the house, a cavalier haunts a bedroom where in life he once hid from searching Roundheads. He was caught, although exactly what then happened to him is unknown. It has been suggested that he was executed at Tyburn but it is difficult to find proof of this. In the room there is a feeling of restlessness and anxiety and something invisible shakes and moves the bed. Anyone staying in this bedroom, after a disturbed and sleepless night, must conclude that the cavalier had an unpleasant end.

The author, Fanny Burney, and her husband General D'Arblay, rented the Hermitage in Bookham from 1793 to 1797. Whether the ghosts which regularly appear at the house have anything to do with her is pure conjecture. Her time here was mainly a happy one, living cosily in a cottage which she described as 'a very small house in the suburbs of a very small village'. Like Slyfield, the Hermitage also has the ghost of a grey lady, but in contrast she radiates a feeling of happiness, possibly reflecting how Fanny Burney felt about her time here.

'I was redecorating the old kitchen when I suddenly felt that somebody else was present near me', a previous owner of the Hermitage recalled. 'I looked up and through the open door, which opened into a room which had previously been the servants' sitting room and into which the old back staircase had descended. I, for a few seconds, was clearly aware of a grey shadowy form of a female wearing a long dress or habit. I felt no sense of fear at all,' the owner continued, 'just an awareness of a link with the past generations. At various times in the house I felt a great sense of being surrounded by an aura of happiness and almost the nearness of departed spirits. I never felt quite alone there. I cannot explain this sensation but it always was a source of satisfaction and a great feeling of continuity.'

Subsequently the ghost was seen by two visitors and also by the owner's son and his brother-in-law. The son described the spectral lady as wearing a grey habit not unlike a nun's habit. She had appeared to him upstairs, coming from a door which had once given access to a servant's bedroom.

The Hermitage also has a ghost dog, small, black, and terrier-like. It may be responsible for the owner's dogs lacking any enthusiasm for descending the stairs into the cellar. 'I was in the kitchen looking out into the garden at the back of the house,' the owner reported, 'and saw what I thought seemed like an Aberdeen terrier. I immediately went out in case a gate had been left open because I feared for my own dog's safety with the volume of traffic along the Lower Road. No gates were left open at the Hermitage and the garden was completely enclosed mostly by a high brick wall which made the garden dog proof.

'I have seen the dog on several other occasions,' he continued, 'as also has my son who states that he has seen the dog walk through the front door, across the hall and out of the garden door, usually in the afternoon and irrespective as to whether the doors were open or closed.'

The owner and his son were not unduly disturbed by the phantom dog's appearances but a gas fitter working at the house was certainly distinctly rattled. He appeared downstairs from the first floor looking 'considerably disturbed', according to the owner. 'He said he had followed a black terrier up the stairs and that the dog had walked across the landing and through a door which was closed. I must emphasise that the Hermitage was always a happy house with a great sense of past family happiness and contentment and I felt a continuing communion with the spirits of former occupants,' said the owner in conclusion.

Bookham has a second ghost dog, described as 'large and rough-haired', and seen lolloping along a track which is no longer there. It is said that the route of the track ran nearly parallel with the Upper Road to cross Downsway at right angles. When the dog meets a house now built across the old route it simply walks straight through it.

Not far from the Hermitage in Lower Road, several bungalows were built in the mid-1920s, most of them with an additional room upstairs in the roof. One of these bungalows is haunted by a happy small girl. She has appeared to those sleeping in the room in the roof and has also been heard by people downstairs as she laughs and plays on her own above them. Needless to say there were no children living in the bungalow when these incidents occurred.

The most famous house in Bookham is Polesden Lacy, a classic of the Edwardian period now in the care of the National Trust. There has been a house here since medieval times but the present building is a 1906 remodelling and enlargement of a house originally built in 1824. Polesden Lacy boasts a couple of ghosts and both relate to the gardens. Firstly, in the

No one has been able to see the face of the mysterious figure clad in a brown cloak at Polesden Lacy. (Author's Collection)

Nun's Walk, the still air is sometimes disturbed by a whirlwind whistling along the track towards the house – a sudden and inexplicable event more frightening in the happening than in the telling. Secondly, a mysterious figure clad in a brown cloak, hood pulled well up over the head obscuring the face, stands on a wooden bridge crossing a sunken road en route to the vegetable gardens. Is it just that the face cannot be seen or is it a macabre fact that it has no face at all?

BRAMLEY

Bramley is an ancient village straddling the Guildford to Horsham road, although little of its past history is visible these days. Its pubs are rightly popular and the place still retains some village atmosphere despite the almost constant traffic passing through.

The parish church is part medieval and part the result of that Victorian religious zeal which led to the 'restoration' of so many of Surrey's churches. From the 13th-century chancel has come the sound of strange music, described as 'medieval'. It echoes through the church and can be heard

Strange music has been heard at Bramley Church. (Author)

outside, even when the church is known to be empty. No explanation for its occurrence has been forthcoming.

A few yards down the High Street from the church a small stream flows under the road. In the doorway of an adjacent shop the ghost of a young lady, a thin wraith of a girl, may make a brief appearance. She is dressed in Victorian clothing, a jilted lover who took her own life. How she did so is open to argument. Some say that she threw herself from an upstairs window, others that she drowned herself in the stream. I opt for the window, rather than the stream where the water is usually no more than a few inches deep.

In Chinthurst Lane near Bramley there have been several reports of a wizened old gypsy woman seen leading a brown horse. Near the stream known as Cranleigh Water both horse and woman simply fade away. Late one night in 1971 an airline pilot was driving home with his daughter down the narrow lane when they were forced to a sudden halt as they came up behind the old lady and her horse. It was a surprise at that time of night but, although he could see both horse and woman, his daughter could only see the horse. The procession of woman, horse and car shuffled slowly down the lane until it reached the road junction near the stream. At that point both horse and woman disappeared.

BURSTOW

Smallfield Place near Burstow is a fine stone manor house with mullioned windows and a roof of Horsham slates. It was originally built about 1600 but altered in 1665, and was the property of the Byshe family, ancestors of the poet, Shelley. Over the succeeding centuries various bits of the house have been demolished, but it is still a building of much character in a style that is quite unusual in Surrey. It is also unusual in the ghosts it has attracted. All are female and there are three of them, two of whom enjoy the comforts of an indoor haunting, but the third appears outside in the gardens dressed in lacy wedding attire. She is seen gliding about before vanishing near a pond. Meanwhile, indoors a woman materialises from a wall as if she has just come through a door that is no longer there and her companion drifts about downstairs dressed in blue. I have not heard of any explanation of the possible origins of these spectral ladies but they all seem to be fairly harmless.

BYFLEET

Byfleet Manor was once a royal hunting lodge which King James I gave to his queen, Anne of Denmark, in 1616. The house of that period has almost disappeared, absorbed by later rebuilding and if Queen Anne were to return today she would not recognise the place.

'There is no ghost-story connected with the Manor House,' stated Frances J Mitchell writing about Byfleet Manor in 1907, 'but one or two half-forgotten legends linger still'.

Several people, both residents and visitors, may not be quite as ready to dismiss their experiences as legends. Within the house the translucent figure of a lady seen moving through the ground floor rooms has been attributed to Queen Anne herself, while, outside, a very small man, perhaps a dwarf, is supposed to wander in the forecourt. Witnesses have described him as being dressed in purple velvet.

Byfleet is situated on the banks of the river Wey and nearby at New Haw it is said that the lock-keeper's cottage has a ghost. Nancy Larcombe, in her excellent book about life on the Wey Navigation, *Captain White's River Life*,

The ghost at the lock cottage at New Haw is very smelly. (Author)

wrote of the cottage that it 'is said, by Capt 'Tiny' Harris, lock-keeper 1959-1982 to be haunted, probably by a lock-keeper's wife who was drowned in the water which flows behind the cottage. On several occasions, in the small hours, he saw a long, shapeless mist passing through the kitchen at the back of the cottage. He said that it was very cold and stank horribly. His wife saw it once and passed out'.

CATERHAM

Jeoffry Spence, who died in 1992, was an indefatigable researcher into the history of his home town of Caterham and he wrote down the facts that old documents revealed and memories recalled. His investigations seemed to bring back to life those who had peopled the past down through the centuries and, wherever the local historian goes in the present, those people seem never far away.

When writing in 1964 about Caterham Court, a house which had been demolished before the Second World War, Spence related the facts which had brought about the tradition that the place had been haunted. Because of a wrangle over inheritance, a daughter was shut up in a room by an angry stepmother. She would have been left to die there by starvation, but was saved by a faithful servant who smuggled food to her. But somehow the daughter 'turned into a ghost,' wrote Spence, 'and used to appear behind her father's chair at midnight'. After the father's death the stepmother 'put a curse on the house so that misfortunes would follow anyone who lived in it'.

Spence found some 'half truths' concerning this story and the Rowed family, who lived at Caterham Court in the 18th century. There was a Katherine Rowed whose father, Henry, did remarry but Katherine survived to at least middle age. As Spence points out, the stepmother '*might* have tried to starve her to death, and it is said that there is no smoke without fire'. It was significant that 'all the later occupiers [of the house] were more or less financially ruined'.

When Jeoffry Spence was young, Caterham Court lay empty and semi-derelict, an exciting playground for a child. As he explored the old house Spence had no thoughts of ghosts in a place that to him always seemed 'most

Caterham Court, where something sinister may have occurred many years ago. (Jean Tooke)

friendly'. One evening he was by himself in the house, sitting halfway up the main staircase pondering over plans for the following day. 'It was quiet, and there was no wind. Quite suddenly there came the sound of a door being quietly, but firmly, closed, and yet somehow seemingly to shake the whole house. Spence felt no fear but 'it was instinctively recognised as the signal to go'. He made his way down a corridor 'with its peeling paper, through a green baize door, past the entrance to the pitch black cellars and out through the kitchen'. He always left the house this way as after sunset there was something unsettling about the front of the house with its dark yews; the door that way was not locked but 'it could never be opened'.

Spence concluded, but without admitting that he had felt a 'presence' there that evening, that it was possible that something 'rather *sinister* had occurred there many years ago, something that imprinted a dark smear on the atmosphere for ever'.

CHEAM

There was a rural village here until much of it was engulfed by a tide of residential building between the two world wars, but there is still the occasional

King Henry VIII's palace at Nonsuch is the source of many ghostly tales. (Surrey Archaeological Society)

old building scattered here and there to hint at what it once was like. One of these is the rectory in Malden Road, solid Georgian brick and haunted.

The ghost here is dressed in 18th-century clothes and makes his appearance in the bedrooms. Some say that he represents a long dead former rector. The extraordinary thing about him is that he has no legs below the knees. This phenomenon is attributed apparently to the fact that the floor levels have been raised and is similar to that witnessed at Wotton House (see page 81).

Nearby was the site of the village of Cuddington but this ancient settlement was swept away by King Henry VIII in 1538. Henry built a magnificent new palace here, unrivalled in its splendour of which none such had existed before, hence its name of Nonsuch. The outside of the palace with its polygonal towers was lavishly decorated in carved and gilded slate with moulded reliefs in dazzling white stucco.

The whole building was demolished around 1685 and very little evidence now survives above ground. Fortunately, the site has not been built on and some of the park survives. An archaeological dig in the late 1950s exposed much of the palace's foundations and cellars, hinting at it what might have been like.

There should be a rich habitat here for ghosts and ghouls and indeed there are a few. A man dressed in a long cloak has been seen regularly about the park and especially at the main entrance. He gazes towards the palace site, a forlorn expression suggested upon his face. Some say (although no evidence has been found to support it) that he is far younger than Nonsuch itself, Victorian in fact, and that he pines for a young girl found murdered in the park.

The site of the banqueting house at Nonsuch stands some distance from the palace and its kitchens, a recipe, I thought, for a lot of cold dinners that would not have pleased King Henry. Actually, the palace was not completed until after Henry's death so Queen Elizabeth I may have had more to complain about in this respect. On certain nights the sounds of happy revelry fuelled by wine and ale drift across the park. Who is to say to which age those shadowy figures of the guests belong?

CHELSHAM

In east Surrey the phenomenon of the phantom coach has been claimed for several places including Chelsham, Warlingham and Coulsdon. I suspect that these three examples are one and the same, and that the story relates to a nasty accident which befell a coach when it plunged into the murky waters of a pond at Slines Green, Chelsham. A search for a pond on old Ordnance Survey maps revealed that, at one time, there were no less than four ponds here. However, the most likely candidate for the accident is the pond at the west end of the green on the south side of the road. An old coach has been witnessed rising from the waters here 'all lit up, with passengers screaming at the windows'.

The story begins on the night of 23rd November 1809. It was a bad night with heavy, incessant rain and winds strong enough to bowl a person over. Enter a coach-driver, one Ted Baxter, a tough, no-nonsense sort of man, a cockney who chewed tobacco and cursed and swore at most things. Baxter was a man whose blood was mostly alcohol and on this particular night witnesses claimed that he was so drunk the 'he could hardly hold the reins when the horses moved off'.

The rain fell in torrents but Baxter was undeterred. Although blinded by the deluge, he whipped up the horses, and faster and faster went the fully-laden coach as it hurtled through the night, swaying violently at every turn of the road. At Slines Green, the driver finally lost control, the coach swerved off the road and plunged straight into a pond. The horses struggled desperately, the screams of terrified passengers rent the air but all to no avail. The coach, six horses, Baxter and his guard, two gentlemen, five ladies and three children sank into the mire and were lost.

Soon after this tragedy, Chelsham people began to report that they has seen a strange coach rumbling down the road towards them, the driver frantically lashing the poor horses with his whip. At the expected moment of impact the coach would either disappear or seem to pass right through the horrified onlooker.

Since then there have been numerous incidents involving the phantom coach. 'It's mostly only seen during a thunderstorm', one villager told a journalist. 'My dear old grandfather saw it once. He often used to tell how as a young man he had seen it come thundering out of the rain, passing right through him.'

One night in 1967 Michael Claxbourn was driving home in his van. Suddenly with a scream he turned the steering wheel hard over, causing the vehicle to lurch off the road and run smack into a tree. Fortunately he was not seriously injured but the details on his insurance claim form made interesting reading. The insurance company thought they had heard all the excuses for an accident that any fertile imagination could possibly conjure up, but Mr Claxbourn's explanation was unique. 'This chap's reason for the accident really takes the biscuit,' said the clerk dealing with the claim. 'He reckons there was no choice but to drive off the road into a tree because an old-fashioned coach and horses came thundering out of the rain straight at him!' The date of the accident was 23rd November.

CHERTSEY

An abbey was founded at Chertsey in about AD 666 and is first recorded in a document written seven years later. This makes Chertsey the oldest recorded place in Surrey. Such a long history must surely be conducive to the establishment of an extensive tradition of ghosts. There must be more grey monks in this part of the county than anywhere else, I thought.

Chertsey Abbey itself has gone. The very fabric of the place was moved, literally stone by stone, in 1538 by Henry VIII who viewed it merely as a handy quarry during his improvements to Hampton Court Palace, just a short boat trip down the river Thames. A portion of the site of one of England's most important abbeys was occupied by an early 19th-century house until it too was demolished in 1964. The abbey's ghosts have gone, but maybe some of them can be found walking the corridors of Hampton Court. Unless, of course, you know better.

The abbey must soon have spawned an adjacent settlement, which survived and prospered beyond the destruction of its raison d'être. It is here, especially inside its pubs and inns, that the stories of ghosts and spectres can be found.

The building occupied by the George in Guildford Street dates from the 15th century and boasts a haunted bedroom. A couple from Somerset, the Cresleys, stayed at the inn around 1965. The night was quite warm and, with a window open for a breath of air, the couple drifted off to sleep. In the middle of the night both were suddenly awoken by the abrupt sensation of something or someone sitting down on the end of their bed. Whatever or whoever it was, it felt distinctly heavy. The Cresleys realised that the room had become strangely cold but, clammy with fear, they dared not look to see what it might be at the foot of the bed. It made no sound. In fact nothing made a sound as a weird oppressive silence blocked out the usual noises of the night. The heavy weight then began to move slowly up the bed.

'The bed seemed to go down in the middle,' Mrs Cresley said later, and, terrified, the couple lay still. Then, as suddenly as it had arrived, the weight was gone. There was a rush of warm air giving the couple the impression that something had gone out through the window.

The landlord and his wife had regularly heard strange noises at night from the empty bar, sounding as if furniture and other objects were being moved around. Now the Cresley's experience focused their attention on that particular bedroom. The sounds of footsteps, creaks and groans came from within the room, even when it was locked and known to be empty.

The sounds of footsteps and groans have been heard coming from an empty room at the George, Chertsey. (Author)

Although still sceptical, it became a part of the pub which they now tended to avoid.

The King's Head, also in Guildford Street, may have inherited one of the Chertsey Abbey's monks. He makes the occasional spectral visit to the barmaid's bedroom, then disappears through the wall where once there was a door. He is supposed to be very smelly!

The Swan in Windsor Street is, allegedly, haunted by a white cat, a spooky feline who apparently belonged to Charles Peace, the notorious Victorian murderer. Peace certainly failed to live up to his name for he shot dead at least two people including a policeman. He was executed at Armley Prison, Leeds, in February 1879 having led the police a merry dance through much of England since 1876, when it is thought he committed his first murder. He may well have visited Chertsey, although the nearest place he is positively known to have been is Peckham, where he was living at the time of his arrest. A music lover and violinist, Peace was a professional burglar. Perhaps his accomplice was a four-footed friend.

CLANDON

Clandon Park is a fine house built between 1713 and 1729 for Thomas, second Lord Onslow, by a Venetian architect, Giacomo Leoni. It is now in the care of the National Trust.

A 'sad whispering wraith in silver brocade' walks through walls at Clandon Park. (B Boyd)

There are reports from here of three ghosts – one is described as a 'hairy faced' man and the other two are female spirits, one dressed in black. However, it is the ghost associated with Thomas Onslow which is the best documented.

'Too long in the body, too large in the posteriors, too short in the legs' was how the author, C E Vulliamy, described Thomas Onslow. The man's unusual anatomical shape and 'waddling progress' led to him acquiring the nickname 'Dicky Ducklegs'. He was 'a man with a plain, smooth, pompous face; not the face of one who is likely to be distinguished in great affairs or brilliant enterprise,' wrote Vulliamy.

While lacking brain and with his only skill described as 'a talent for buffoonery', Thomas showed a certain shrewdness as well as meanness when it came to money. He was a rich man but he added to his wealth by marrying an heiress, Elizabeth Knight, whose family had acquired their fortune from estates in Jamaica.

A surviving portrait of Elizabeth was described by Vulliamy as showing her as 'neither attractive nor ugly, rather homely than aristocratic, and certainly unfashionable'. Her father-in-law, the famous Speaker of the House of Commons, Arthur Onslow, described her as 'a woman of the truest goodness of mind and heart I ever knew'. Much of her money, it is said, went into the building of Clandon Park but the poor woman had but a brief time as mistress of the house for she died in 1731. Tradition has it that Elizabeth was unhappy at Clandon where she found no peace of mind and probably no love either. Possibly, she felt used, as it seemed that Dicky Ducklegs had wanted just two things from his wife, a fortune and a male heir, both of which she ably provided.

Elizabeth still walks the corridors and grounds of Clandon Park. Her ghost has been described as 'a dark lady dressed in cream satin'. She has been spotted carrying what appears to be a large knife, which seems somewhat at odds with what we know about her character. She has walked right through the front wall of the house, a gliding figure who visits each room in turn before resuming her garden rambles outside the back wall. Maybe she is still searching for the happiness that eluded her in life. C E Vulliamy's version of the haunting is much more in keeping with the lady as she was in life. In *The Onslow Family* the author wrote of Elizabeth's appearance on the gallery above the hall where 'her pale unfashionable spirit wanders in the gentlest way, a sad whispering wraith in silver brocade...'

COBHAM

In the cold early hours of a morning in December 1966, four members of a pop group known as 'The Peter Bs' were in their van, returning to London from a gig at a club in Portsmouth. Near Cobham one of them suddenly yelled out, pointing to something that he had spotted gliding along the pavement. Then the other three band members spotted a figure dressed like a military man in a greatcoat which was 'a curious mixture of yellow, white and grey with a luminous glow'. The figure was about 100 yards in front of them when first seen. It was marching towards them with head erect but where its eyes should have been, there were only black sockets. Although eyeless, the ghoul seemed to stare vacantly straight ahead. For ten seconds or so it came on as the band members froze in their seats and then it simply 'wheeled off and vanished'.

Later the four gave more detailed accounts of this unnerving incident to a *Sunday Mirror* reporter. 'As we rounded a bend I saw what appeared to be a tall man gliding along and staring straight ahead', said guitar player, Pete Green. 'I could see the side of his face but couldn't really see any expression. It was blank. It didn't dawn on me at first that this was not human. But it stared straight ahead, without looking at our van, and it moved so slowly, mechanically. It seemed to have an unusual stride ... the arms were moving steadily. Like something out of a horror film.'

'It wasn't an ordinary bloke,' said the band's leader and driver, Peter Bardens. 'He was abnormally big and radiated a pale light. I shuddered and gripped the steering wheel, I was temporarily out of my mind. It was horrible. The whole thing seemed greyish-whitish-yellowish. Its eyes were either closed, or the sockets could have been empty.'

'The man was in his fifties,' Bardens continued, 'nearly seven foot tall, I would say, and he did not wear a hat. But his great long overcoat seemed to go almost down to his feet. Or it could have been a kind of shroud', he concluded.

It was drummer, Mick Fleetwood, who got the best view of the spectre as he was sitting on the left-hand side of the front seat, nearest to the footpath. 'When I saw its long expressionless face, forlorn, drawn, and staring straight ahead, I let out a yell. It was an old face. Could have been about sixty. The whole figure, including the head and the hair was a light colour, fluorescent grey. The coat was the same sort of length my father used to wear. A sort of field coat almost to the ankles.'

The experience had clearly upset the four musicians. 'I have never seen anything like this before and I never want to again. It was horrifying,' said one of them.

But who was this terrifying apparition seen that dark night at Cobham? The description was very similar to an apparition seen by others in the same area, a tall figure dressed in a military field coat. This wraith has been linked to Field-Marshall Jean Louis Ligonier, who lived at Cobham Park, then known as Down Place. Ligonier, who died in 1770 aged 89, had an amazing career in the army. According to Cobham local historian David Taylor, he took part in 23 general actions and nineteen sieges without receiving so much as a scratch. He was with Marlborough and fought in all the great battles against the French during the reign of Queen Anne and, in 1757, was created Commander-in-Chief of the British Army. Although he never married, Ligonier was infamous for his liking for young girls and boasted a harem of at least four of them even into old age! However, there seems no particular reason for linking him with the ghoulish apparition seen by the four musicians, but maybe his quest for young ladies still drives him on!

There have been several unexplained happenings at Cobham church. (Author)

Cobham is really two villages, Church Cobham with the ancient church of St Andrew down by the river Mole, and Street Cobham, which straddles the Portsmouth Road. Here there was once a plethora of inns and public houses to cater for the thirst of travellers upon the old turnpike. One of these pubs was known as the Tartar and it was from here one chilling wet night in 1947 that a van driver found himself involuntarily stopping to pick up a girl waiting by the roadside. The girl got in without a word and he drove off, strangely silenced by her presence, a cold fear beginning to spread throughout his body. When he reached Church Street, still without a word having been spoken, his van suddenly stopped. The girl got out and walked away in silence, taking the man's jacket to keep her dry. The man drove on as if in a dream. A week later when he was again in Church Street he sought out the home of the girl in the hope of getting his jacket back. Shortly afterwards he found himself being led by the girl's father to her grave in the churchyard, where he found his jacket lying over a gravestone. His hitchhiker of a week ago had died ten years before.

This is a classic ghost story which can be found repeated in many places throughout England. You will find the story in more detail in my book, *The*

Ghosts of Surrey, but is it legend, fact or fiction? Some parts of the Cobham version are good but others do not, perhaps, stand too much scrutiny.

St Andrew's church has a ghost and once again it is that old friend, the blue donkey, who has put in an appearance, this time to a party of bell-ringers as they walked through the churchyard. I am mystified as to why the ghost of a donkey is so commonplace in Surrey and why such an unearthly colour?

Lime House in Church Street, Cobham, was the scene of a very peculiar incident during the early 1920s, which was experienced by a very young girl who never forgot it even as she grew into old age. She related these events to her husband who found the details sufficiently strange to warrant recording.

'Believe it or not, she remembers an incident [at Lime House] when she was still in her cot. She awoke and found herself surrounded by a party of evil looking men at a cock fight' said the husband in 2001. 'She screamed her head off ,' he continued, 'and her mother and a friend hurried up to see what was wrong. They walked straight through the men, and the cock-fight and everyone disappeared. My wife has always been convinced Lime House must have been haunted,' he concluded.

This is a very weird incident indeed for which there seems little explanation. Perhaps, it was merely a dream but who can say where dreams might end and consciousness begin.

CRANLEIGH

During the last hundred years or so the village of Cranleigh has grown so much that there are now continual arguments over whether it qualifies to be called a town. It is certainly a busy place these days despite the railway having come and gone.

In 1950 the rector of Cranleigh, the Reverend H L Johnston, must have been pleased to receive an interesting letter for inclusion in the parish magazine. It was always difficult to fill those monthly pages and he must have had many other more pressing matters to occupy his time. Of the letter's contents the rector commented that it would 'doubtless intrigue others as much as it has interested me'.

'The other day, after passing through Cranleigh on the way to Bramley,' the writer reported, 'I saw, 200 yards ahead of the car, a man on a penny-farthing bicycle in a well-worn mackintosh and slouch hat; this unusual sight I watched carefully. As we gained on him he mounted a side grass-bordered path and, as the bonnet of the car came abreast of him, he vanished. There was no gate or road there, but a few sparse trees. Not being psychic, I am writing to ask if you would kindly tell me if you know of any tragedy there in the 'penny-farthing' days.' Unfortunately for the rector, his parishioners were not intrigued and remained completely silent on this mysterious matter. There were no further comments or replies in subsequent issues of the parish magazine and a mystery it must remain. Unless, of course, someone out there has kept the answer to themselves.

To the south of Cranleigh lies Baynards Park, but it is now a park bereft of its house, which was demolished after a fire in 1979. The house was built by Sir George More of Loseley in the late 16th century but much altered in Victorian times. The earliest known reference to the place is dated 1447 and there was probably another house here before Sir George More bought Baynards in 1587, but the exact location of this earlier house is not known.

Baynards has been associated with the ghost of Sir Thomas More, author of *Utopia*, who was executed in July 1535 by Henry VIII. More (no relation to the Mores of Loseley) could not accept Henry's divorce from Catherine of Aragon,

Baynards Park near Cranleigh, where the headless cadaver of Sir Thomas More has been seen. (Surrey Archaeological Society)

nor his consequent break with the Catholic Church. As a result he was imprisoned in the Tower and later beheaded. His end was a gruesome affair. The executioner, the infamous Jack Ketch, took five blows with the axe and even then had to finish cutting the head off with his knife.

More's body was buried in St Peter's church at the Tower but what happened to his head? Firstly it was parboiled, as was the usual custom, and then stuck on a pole and exhibited on London Bridge. One report said that by November 1535 the head had turned black and had been thrown into the Thames. However, it was also recorded that his daughter, Margaret, managed to obtain her father's head only a month or so after it had been stuck on the pole. She preserved it in spices until her death in 1544 and it has been suggested that the head was then buried with her at Chelsea. Another possibility is that it was buried with her husband at Canterbury in 1578. In yet another version of events it was passed to More's granddaughter, Elizabeth. She married Sir Edward Bray, who owned Baynards from 1558 until the 1580s. If this is so, then the head would have been brought to the earlier house at Baynards, not the house built by Sir George More after 1587.

Wherever his head ended up, the ghost of Sir Thomas More has been claimed for Baynards. It appeared on a number of occasions before the destruction of the house in 1979, a ghoulish, blood-stained, headless cadaver tottering about the rambling pile. It might have had better luck at Canterbury or Chelsea.

CROYDON

Despite its modern appearance with tower blocks and roads roaring with traffic, Croydon is an ancient place. It was here, probably in the 12th century, that the archbishops of Canterbury established a summer residence, where the air was sweet and the clear chalk-stream waters of the river Wandle bubbled out of the ground. Substantial parts of the palace still survive and for many years have been used as a school. It comes as no surprise to find that the place is haunted.

An Elizabethan lady once regularly appeared at the top of a staircase. She was much troubled, and was seen crying and repeatedly wringing her hands. Those who witnessed this spectre reported that despair was written all over her face. The staircase has subsequently been removed but apparently the whole area has a discomforting feel, especially after dark. An explanation suggests that this 16th-century woman was pregnant when she committed suicide. She now returns searching for the child that never was. She may have something to

A troubled Elizabethan lady walks the remnants of Croydon Palace.
(Surrey Archaeological Society)

do with the cries of a baby heard coming from the chapel where there is also a feeling of unhappiness and despair.

I have traced a strange tale of a haunting which originated in the late 1940s but I have not been able to trace the exact location in Croydon. A young watchmaker had lost his life in a motorcycle accident but his spirit returned to make its presence felt in a most unusual way – it started to operate an electric lathe where the deceased had worked in the family business. One day, shortly after the tragedy, this lathe suddenly burst into life, then stopped, and then gave what were described as 'three sharp movements as if someone had momentarily depressed the pedal which actuated the driving motor'.

Early one morning, not long after this strange event, a policemen called at the family home to say that there was something moving in their shop and that some equipment sounded as if it were running. A member of the family then accompanied the policemen back to the shop and they found the lathe running at an alarming rate. They were totally mystified as to how this could be happening as the lathe was disconnected from its drive motor. The machine was going at such a speed that various small tools left on the workbench the night before had been thrown to the floor. After the two had watched the machine for some time it suddenly stopped.

In the family home there was also some unnerving poltergeist activity. The lights kept being turned on and off even though all the occupants of the house could be accounted for. An electrician called in the next day but failed to find any faults at all. Then, just as suddenly as the poltergeist had arrived, it departed, and the family were left to grieve their loss in peace.

The Sandrock pub in Upper Shirley Road has two ghosts apparently. One is said to be a landlady from the past who returns to supervise the running of 'her' pub. She terrorised one barmaid to such an extent that the girl gave up her job. The second ghost appears as an bearded old man, who gives the impression of being a preacher. Perhaps he is endeavouring to save the souls of present customers from the demon drink!

There was a great fire at Croydon parish church in 1867, one consequence of which was that the tomb of Gilbert Sheldon, Archbishop of Canterbury from 1663 until his death in 1677, was completely destroyed. The destruction obviously caused the spirit of the late archbishop much distress for it started to haunt the church. The ghost was seen by many people, usually at about a

*The fire at Croydon church in 1867 disturbed the spirit of Archbishop Sheldon.
(Surrey Archaeological Society)*

quarter to six in the evening, wandering sorrowfully about the church. These incidents continued until 1960, when the archbishop's tomb was restored and his spirit was once more at rest. There have since then been no further reports of his ghost.

Frances D Stewart, in her comprehensive study of Croydon's many ghosts, *Around Haunted Croydon*, related a curious tale of a haunting at Croydon hospital. A night-duty nurse was sitting at her desk attending to some paper work when she heard the swing doors at the entrance to the ward open and a trolley being wheeled in. Then she heard the clatter of cups and the sound of a tap being turned on in the kitchen.

The nurse got up and went to investigate but, of course, there was no one there. She returned from the kitchen and quietly went round the ward checking the patients. There was one patient in particular whose health was cause for a great deal of concern. When the nurse reached his bed, she saw that he appeared to be awake. As she re-arranged his bed clothes, she asked him gently if he would like a cup of tea. 'No thanks, I've just had one from the nurse dressed in white,' came the whispered reply. There was no such nurse on duty that night. Next morning the patient died. The night nurse related her strange experience to other members of staff and was told that the ghostly nurse often returned to what had once been her ward. She usually came when a patient had not long for this world.

During its years of existence, Croydon Airport has witnessed many of the pioneer flights that were such great landmarks in the history of aviation, including those of the heroine of long distance flying, Amy Johnson. It was inevitable that the aerodrome would also be connected with those tragedies that were regularly a feature of the early days of flying. In the period between the two world wars, pilots did not have the benefits of accurate weather forecasting or the computer-based navigational aids which are a routine part of everyday air travel today. If the fog came down during your flight, the results might be fatal. This is, in fact, exactly what happened to a Dutch pilot sometime during the 1930s who took off in the expectation that the forecasts of good weather were correct. However, shortly after take-off, he ran into a wall of impenetrable fog. Imagine the horror as the plane flew on completely blind, the pilot straining to pick out any feature on the ground below that might help him to fix his position. He could make out nothing and then the ground was suddenly there and he was dead. A couple of weeks later, an Imperial Airways pilot sat alone plotting the course of his next flight. The weather forecast was good and all the signs were that his aircraft would be leaving on time. The pilot's concentration was then interrupted by a voice which came from behind him.

'You can't take off. The weather's just the same as when I did,' said a voice.

The pilot turned round to question the speaker and there stood the figure of the recently dead Dutchman, whom the pilot had known well. The figure said nothing more and then faded away. The pilot was in a quandary and very shocked by this strange visitation but, although the skies were still clear, the decision was taken to cancel the flight. A little later a pea-souper of a fog descended upon the airport.

The circumstances of the incident seem to relate to the crash of a Dutch KLM DC2 airliner which hit a house in Hillcrest Road, Purley, on a foggy morning in December 1936. Of the fourteen people on board only two survived. The dead included a former prime minister of Sweden and a Spaniard, Juan de la Cierva, inventor of the autogiro, the world's first operational vertical take-off aircraft.

Croydon Airport closed in 1959. It had played an important role during the Second World War and before that it had been the first London airport. Now the aircraft were getting too big for its runways and the whole place was hemmed in by residential estates. The site of the airport was soon redeveloped and during this work the ghosts of the place were much disturbed.

At one of the building developments, workman who were sleeping on site were woken by the sound of a large group of people singing. Could these singers be the re-enactment of a wartime NAAFI concert or were their cheery melodies coming from an air raid shelter, where the erstwhile occupants sat patiently waiting for the all clear signal? In another incident, workman were surprised by a motorcyclist who appeared from nowhere driving towards them at high speed. The rider crouching over his machine was dressed in an airman's flying jacket, and as the motorbike roared past, it glanced back at the transfixed workman. Their horror was obvious – the airman had no face.

DORKING

Dorking, as befits any ancient town in Surrey, has its share of ghouls and hauntings but not, I think, as many to rival Guildford or Farnham, unless, of course, you know better!

The town's most famous inn, the White Horse, should not be without a ghost of its own, and this is, indeed, true. The inn is haunted by a high calibre spectre who appears sporting what have been described as 'robes of state' with a 'ducal crown' atop his aristocratic head. It says something for the status of the inn that such nobility should visit so regularly even after death.

In West Street there is a shop with a plaque fixed to the wall proudly

The White Horse at Dorking plays host to a high status spectre. (Author)

announcing that here was once the home of William Mullins, who sailed with the Pilgrim Fathers to America in 1620 aboard the *Mayflower*. The brave immigrants reached the coast of their promised land in December of that year, but disease was rife among them and, just two months after making landfall, William Mullins was dead. There seems little to link the recent hauntings of William Mullins' home with the man himself, but perhaps there is a connection. The shop is haunted by a young girl wearing a full-length dress of the usual grey. Mullins sailed with his wife and a son and daughter, but only the daughter, Priscilla, survived the initial stages of the colony. Perhaps it is Priscilla who has returned to haunt her last home in England. She has been heard moving items around upstairs and shutting a door which had long-since been removed. One member of staff encountered the spectre of the girl upon the stairs as it gently pushed past her and disappeared. The girl has been thought responsible for various incidents of poltergeist activity. Objects have been mysteriously moved or have inexplicably been seen to rise up and then crash to the floor. On one occasion a picture was taken off its hook on the wall and left on the stairs. The spirit here has been reported as not one to induce fear but rather the opposite.

This is in contrast to events at another house in Dorking, which was once described as being 'disagreeably haunted'. Tenants of this rambling house came and went in rapid succession and at times the house stood empty. Any attempt to sleep in one of the bedrooms was fraught with all sorts of terrors. This included the vision of a horribly distorted face, floating above the bed, which would then suddenly spout water at its now quaking victim. Is this is the first example of ghostly dribble that I have encountered?

Around the outskirts of Dorking there are a number of recorded hauntings. On a hill nearby, our old friend, the spectre of a donkey, sometimes glows, but not, apparently, in blue on this occasion. On the Dorking bypass many a motorist has been shocked by the translucent image of a horse and rider that charges across the road. It is presumably following an ancient track.

The famous beauty spot of Box Hill looks down upon the town of Dorking and here lies the burial place of Peter Labelliere. The circumstances surrounding his final resting place are as eccentric as the life of the man himself. He came to live in Dorking sometime after 1763, a deeply religious man, who was the author of various religious tracts with titles that included *The Christian Political Mousetrap*. He forbade his landlady's children from burning any piece of paper which bore the name of God or Jesus. Generous to a fault, he would give away his shoes or coat to any pauper he met on his rambles around the town. Over the years Labelliere became increasingly

Peter Labelliere is buried upside down on Box Hill near Dorking. (Author)

careless of his appearance and personal hygiene. As a result, he was nicknamed 'The Walking Dunghill' but most of the inhabitants of the town looked on him as just a harmless crank.

Labelliere found Box Hill an ideal place for his meditations and was often seen striding through the woodlands there reciting prayers as he went along. On one of these walks he tripped and fell, landing upon some spike that gouged out an eye. It was here on the same spot that he chose to be buried and when he died in 1800, the good people of Dorking ensured that all his wishes were fulfilled. He was placed in the grave upside down, some say because he thought that the world was so topsy-turvy that when it came right, he would be the right way up. Others consider that he asked to be buried in this way because that was how St Peter was crucified. Labelliere called for no religious rites at his funeral and asked that his landlady's children should dance upon his grave. It seems he wished to emphasize that the journey to his maker would be a happy affair, not a melancholy one. There was a packed crowd at the funeral and in subsequent years many Dorking people returned to the spot to picnic and celebrate the life of a lovable eccentric.

Since then there have been many reports over the years of the sighting on Box Hill of a strangely dressed one-eyed man striding through the woods or standing on the grassy slopes, his eye set towards the magnificence of the southerly view. Sometimes the man wears a three-cornered hat and a blue coat and is heard muttering prayers to himself as he walks, head down against a strange cold wind that marks his coming. He is there one minute and then is not. His words '... for Jesus Christ's sake, save us and the whole race of mankind, as the returning prodigal' hang in the air long after he has gone.

ESHER

Jane and Anna Maria Porter were the daughters of an Irish army surgeon who had served with the Inniskilling Dragoons during the early years of the Napoleonic Wars. Their father died at a comparatively young age, leaving his wife and daughters only a small income upon which to survive. The depleted family moved to Thames Ditton where the widow rented Boyle Farm Cottage. Fortunately for Mrs Porter she soon had no need to worry financially as both daughters turned out to be accomplished writers, especially Jane. In 1803 her first novel entitled *Thaddeus of Warsaw* was a great success and this was soon followed by *The Scottish Chiefs*, a novel still considered by some to be a minor classic.

By the early 1820s both Jane and her mother had developed health problems and a move was made from Thames Ditton to the higher ground of Esher. The good air, the heaths and pines, and the general attractiveness of the village of Esher, had already brought the rich, royal and famous to live here. For their new home, the Porters chose a fairly small but pleasant house situated in the upper part of the High Street. It was called Alderlands and has survived to this day, although long since converted into shops.

With their reputation established it was not surprising that Alderlands was often busy with visitors and friends. Amongst these was Admiral Nagle, a genial Irishman, who strolled down almost every day from his home at Moore Place. The Admiral had led an eventful life during 24 years in the navy and was a great favourite with George IV. He was known for his 'rollicking Irish humour' and his ability to tell a good story and was appointed to the position of groom of the bedchamber in 1820. In 1825 he bought Moore Place and retired to the peace and quiet of Esher.

Life passed happily at Alderlands. Both Jane and Anna continued their writing, although Jane's earlier successes were not repeated. One evening in March 1830, the Admiral entered Alderlands for what appeared to be a normal evening visit for a cup of tea and conversation. He walked into the main room of the house and seated himself at a table. His face was white. He looked ill and gave no reply to his hosts' greetings but sat staring straight ahead, anxiety in his eyes. When Anna asked him what was wrong, he simply rose from his chair, walked out of the room and out of the house without saying a single word. This was most uncharacteristic as he always had a good story to tell about something or other.

Anna sent her servant to follow the Admiral to make sure that all was well. The servant soon returned with the startling news that, as soon as the Admiral had stepped out of the Porter's home, he had disappeared. When the servant

Moore Place, Esher, where Admiral Nagle died in 1830. (Author)

enquired at Moore Place, she was told the tragic news that the old man had died about an hour before.

Anna always insisted that she had indeed seen Admiral Nagle enter Alderlands that evening. It is unclear whether Jane also saw the apparition but she later related the story to the author John Ingram, who published a brief account of it in his book *The Haunted Homes and Family Traditions of Great Britain*.

This last visit of Admiral Nagle came almost as a warning to the Porter family, his anxiety suggesting bad times ahead. Indeed, they were not long in coming. In 1831 Mrs Porter died, a loss which deeply affected the sisters. With their literary success rapidly on the wane, Alderlands now seemed cold and dead, and shortly after their mother's death, the sisters gave up the house and moved to Bristol. In 1832 tragedy struck again, when Anna contracted typhoid and died. Jane lived on, all inspiration gone, but she did manage to grind out two more novels. Neither brought her back into the fold of the successful and in 1850 she died, lonely and forgotten, at the age of 76.

EWELL

The history at Ewell begins when prehistoric man first took advantage of the clear springs which bubble out of the ground around here to form the Hogsmill River. The Romans built a major settlement here which became an important stopping place for travellers on Roman Stane Street. Nearby, at Nonsuch (see page 19), Henry VIII built a magnificent palace. Ewell still retains something of a village atmosphere, despite a tide of residential development in the 1930s which threatened to engulf it. A number of ancient buildings have survived including the village gaol. Therefore, it is not surprising to find a ghost or two here where men and women have lived and died through many centuries.

Near the gaol is number 26 High Street, a building with origins probably in the 16th century but undoubtedly on the site of something even older. Over the years there have been many unaccountable disturbances here. One tenant reported the sensation of someone or something brushing past them on the narrow stairs. It was claimed to be a ghost who is active only on a Friday evening, usually between 6 pm and 7 pm. The manifestation includes the

A ghost coach is heard outside the King William IV pub at Ewell. (Author)

regular sound of heavy footsteps crossing the floor of the upstairs front room while several visitors have sensed a strong 'presence', particularly on the stairs. The hauntings are thought to be connected with Nonsuch and there is claimed to be a tunnel connecting the house to Henry's palace. If it exists at all it is possibly only a drain.

The William IV pub was a favourite watering hole of mine when I helped on an archaeological dig in the gardens behind the pub during the late 1960s. We uncovered a great deal of Roman material here and also many later features and artefacts. These included hundreds of clay tobacco pipes thrown out after use in the pub itself. Some were so clean that you could almost see the moisture on the mouthpiece left from the lips of the smoker a century or more ago, and in the imagination you could hear a coach as it pulled to a halt beside the hostelry and weary passengers dismounting. The strong emotions and sensations of those now gone can be re-enacted and such is the case outside this pub: the rumble of coach wheels and the clatter of the horses hooves are often heard. The phantom coach halts but cannot be seen and after a while it departs again in the direction of the old route towards London.

The Pre-Raphaelite artist William Holman Hunt stayed with his uncle at Ewell and he told of a haunting which he experienced just outside the village late one night in 1847. Some years later, he recalls 'arriving by the last train from London at the Ewell Station [now Ewell East] on the other side of the village, the station master shut up his office and came out with a lantern to walk home. I accompanied him, being glad of his light. When we had entered under some heavy trees I cautioned him that some white creature, probably an animal, was advancing towards us. "It will be sure to get out of our way," he said, and walked on unfalteringly.'

'Yet I kept my eyes riveted on the approaching being,' continued Hunt. 'When we had come nearer I interrupted our idle chat, saying "but it is steadily coming towards us". He turned up his gaze and was stopped by what he saw. The mysterious midnight roamer proved to be no brute, but had the semblance of a stately, tall man wrapped in white drapery round the head and down to the feet. Stopping within five paces from us, he seemed to look through me with his solemn gaze. Would he speak? I wondered.'

At this point Holman Hunt was brave enough to take a long look at the phantom. 'Was his ghostly clothing merely vapour? I peered at it; it seemed too solid for this, and yet not solid enough for earthly garb. We both stood paralysed and expectant. Then the figure deliberately marched to our left, making a half-circle around us, till he regained the line he had been travelling upon, and paced majestically forward. Clutching my companion's arm, I said, "What is it?" His reply was "It's a ghost".'

The artist Holman Hunt saw a strange spectre after he got off a train at Ewell,
now Ewell East, station in 1847. (Author)

The artist was all for following this strange spectre but the station master
had seen enough and, unsurprisingly, was not prepared to give up his lantern.
'Had I dared to follow it without a light, the striking of the church clock would
have reminded me that I was already fully late ... and I left the mystery
unsolved. At a point where our road met the village, we came upon two sober
men, of whom we asked what person it was that had lately passed them. They
said they had been standing there ten minutes, and nobody had gone by.'

FARNHAM

My researches into the ghosts of Surrey have convinced me that
Farnham must be amongst the spookiest towns in the county.
Most places have their grey ladies and ominous monks but this
attractive town, with its imposing castle and streets lined with Georgian
houses, is home to almost every ghostly apparition that could be imagined. For
centuries Farnham Castle was home to the Bishops of Winchester and the
town saw more activity during the Civil War than anywhere else in Surrey. It

also developed as one of England's most important corn markets and in more recent times became a centre for the growing of that most essential ingredient of good beer, hops.

Farnham Castle was built in the early 12th century by Henry de Blois, Bishop of Winchester and brother of King Stephen. However, much of what is visible today dates from later in the same century with various additions, particularly in the 15th century. In 1643 the Royalists made a half-hearted attempt to capture the castle from General Waller's Roundheads and later the keep was blown up. Great chunks of it still stand, teetering above the slopes of the castle mound. Many visitors have felt a strange presence at the entrance to the keep and a 'strange psychic atmosphere' pervades its ruined guardroom, where a mere shadow, perhaps a woman in medieval clothes, has been seen.

Many visitors have felt a strange presence at the entrance to the keep of Farnham Castle. (Author's Collection)

The castle remained a palace of the Bishops of Winchester until 1927 and reports of ghosts have been a regular occurrence here over the years. The apparition of a knight clad in full armour has been seen lurching about. His unsteady walk is perhaps not surprising considering the huge weight of the average suit of armour. A lady in white, who glides through certain corridors at midnight, has been suggested as a portent of the death of someone associated with the castle. She appeared to three people in three separate incidents shortly before news reached the castle of the death in a riding accident of Bishop Wilberforce. Samuel Wilberforce had become Bishop of Winchester in 1869. In 1873, he was riding near Abinger Hammer when he was thrown from his horse and killed. At the moment of death Wilberforce made a fleeting appearance at a window at Wotton House, a mile or two from his place of death, but his spirit failed to travel as far as Farnham.

The castle does, however, have its resident ghostly cleric, said to be Bishop Morley, who died in 1684. He spent a great deal of money restoring the bishop's palace following the damage caused during the Civil War but is said to have lead a Spartan existence, rising at five in the morning, summer and winter, and eating only one meal a day. Generous to a fault, it is said that he ended his days in a tiny cell-like room at the foot of a staircase in what is known as Fox's Tower, named after another bishop. Some accounts have him spending the last 20 years of his life in a coffin, receiving food through a small hole but my researches have found nothing to support this exaggerated view. Now Morley wanders about the place 'as if looking for something' and strange noises at night have been attributed to him. A bell removed long ago is struck once more and footsteps are heard crossing the bishop's private apartments. Footsteps are also heard at night on the road outside, crunching on loose gravel despite the fact that the road up to the castle has been tarmacked for many years. Perhaps it is the bishop taking his nightly constitutional.

Bishop Morley, the knight and the lady are not alone in walking the corridors and halls of this ancient building. On a staircase a little dancing girl in medieval garb returns to the spot where she had collapsed and died, and phantom monks or clerics have been reported in many parts of the castle and its grounds. A ghostly procession of monks, their heads bowed, trudges silently across the lawn below Fox's Tower, and in 1973 a figure dressed in grey appeared on a staircase outside the Great Hall. A solid looking image, moving strangely, which glided towards a window and vanished. Fifty years earlier a servant had seen what she described as 'a tall man, dressed in a brown habit' at the end of the gallery in the Great Hall. On his head he wore a cap reminiscent of a skull-cap. In the so-called minstrels gallery, also in the Great Hall, the same servant reported seeing a monk-like figure; others too have felt a claustrophobic sensation of fear and oppression here.

The bishop's palace and castle on its lofty elevation brought wealth to Farnham and the place grew into a substantial town by 1664, second only to Guildford. The town itself is not to be outdone by the plethora of ghosts which kept the bishops company up on the hill, for it has plenty of its own. The fine houses of Castle Street, which lie in the shadow of Bishop Morley's home, have several resident ghosts. At number 68, a variety of strange noises, including heavy footfalls, have been attributed to 'George', a jilted lover who hanged himself. Another house in the street has an apparition in the form of a young gentleman 'dressed for the hunt', who appears in one of the bedrooms. Meanwhile, out in the street, a phantom coach disgorges a drunken figure, who then lurches across the road to vanish as he enters a house.

In 1974 a former jeweller's shop at the bottom of Castle Street was undergoing renovation. Here a wispy old man with a fixed stare appeared, raising the suspicion among the workmen that he was a spy sent to check on progress: a fact hotly denied by their employer. The old man's dress included a jeweller's leather apron and, when the men were shown a photograph of the deceased previous owner, ghost and jeweller proved to be a match.

The long defunct Castle Theatre was once described by Sir Michael Redgrave as 'the most haunted he had ever worked in'. Repeats of brief moments of its previous incarnations were regularly experienced by those working at the theatre. The building had been a roller-skating rink early last century and later a cinema, before becoming a theatre just before the Second World War. Various sounds and poltergeist activity seem to have been experienced here throughout much of the building's history. Excited skaters continued to whirl around the floor, despite the rows of seats blocking their path and a poltergeist was accused of meddling with cinema equipment. Later, a wandering thespian, perhaps still in search of the fame that had eluded him in life, walked the boards once more.

Architecturally, West Street is the jewel in Farnham's crown, but the street also has no trouble in matching Castle Street for ghosts. On dark, wet, winter nights the figure of an old man runs down the street at a surprising speed for his apparent age, skimming past the unwary, only to disappear at a doorway. Perhaps the most well known of Farnham's ghosts is the 'black dog of West Street', which has been seen in a house here on many occasions and also in the street. He has been spotted inside number 90 West Street, running down the stairs when the householder's own dogs were fast asleep in their baskets. On another occasion he appeared in the kitchen, a docile wisp of canine spirit who doesn't even bark! In the same house odd noises like the sound of rolling drums have been heard and the image of an old woman wearing a nightdress appeared in the bathroom, which was once a bedroom. Perhaps she is the black dog's owner looking for her lost friend.

Number 68 West Street is haunted by the ghost of a small girl who is described as 'very plain', aged about 15 and under 5 ft in height.

68 West Street, Farnham, is haunted by the ghost of a small girl. (Author)

Vernon House now forms part of Farnham's public library but, as a private house, it once played a small part in one of the most momentous events in British history. On 19th December 1648, King Charles I was taken from the Isle of Wight under heavy guard to his trial in London. On the following night, this unusual band of travellers stayed in Farnham, where the king was lodged at Henry Vernon's house in West Street. It is said that many local people, anxious to get a sight of their king, crowded into the room where Charles took his supper. We are not told of their attitude to their hapless monarch but, when he departed the following morning for Bagshot, he presented the Vernons with a morning cap as a memento. Five weeks later the king was dead. With the house's august history it is not surprising that the shadowy figure of a well-dressed man of the 17th century has been seen on the stairs and that library staff have spoken of one particular room where a 'strong presence' is felt, accompanied by the perfume of violets.

Just down the road from Vernon House is Lion and Lamb Yard, a reminder of one of Farnham's famous inns, and several ghostly manifestations have been reported here. A woman dressed in old-fashioned riding clothes has appeared, and footsteps have been heard clattering upon a long-removed flight of stairs. A lady 'in fancy dress' was seen through a window at a café here and, whilst she was clearly visible to some customers, others could see nothing. Yet another female apparition, dressed in grey, was seen sitting at a café table in the courtyard waiting to be served. When the waitress approached the lady to take her order, she simply vanished. Tradition says that it is once again the strong emotion of unrequited love that draws her back to Farnham.

The Lion and Lamb is just one of a number of Farnham inns associated with ghosts. The Hop Bag Inn, Downing Street, had a long history of hauntings until it was demolished in the early 1990s. Several years ago, however, a lady visitor staying at the inn was awoken in the middle of the night by the clatter of horses' hooves and the rumble of coach wheels. She listened as the vehicle came to a stop in the yard below and then, curiosity getting the better of the comforts of a warm bed, the guest got up, parted the curtains slightly and looked down into the yard. It was empty.

The Bush Hotel has a spectral housekeeper, who apparently came to a sticky end, and is sometimes seen in the corridor near room 18. She has been known to move the furniture about and remove keys but otherwise causes the guests no trouble.

A house in East Street was haunted by a female figure clad in a full-skirted dress, presumably of the Victorian period, who first appeared to the lady of the house one night when she was lying in bed. The phantom stood in the bedroom doorway but when the light was switched on it was gone. Over a period of many years it was seen by various family members and sometimes there were footsteps and knocks. Strangely, it seemed to appear with the impending arrival of a baby to someone associated with the house, leading to the suggestion that it was a phantom midwife or a jealous childless wife.

During the Second World War, firewatchers had the unenviable task of sitting through the night atop the tower of the mainly 15th century parish church of St Andrew. Shock and confusion were caused on one occasion when rows of lights were seen below moving around the building. These points of light looked for all the world, or the next, like a candle-lit procession making its way to the church entrance. When the church was checked it was, of course, empty. This incident may have something to do with the images seen by a woman praying alone at the back of the church. She witnessed what appeared to be the celebration of an ancient High Mass, the congregation half filling the church, shadowy figures, some moving around, with a gold-clad cleric and his assistants at the altar. A strange semi-transparent veil, which slowly descends to separate off the chancel, has also been seen in Farnham church. Wispy figures and shadows appear to move around behind it at the altar. Visitors standing

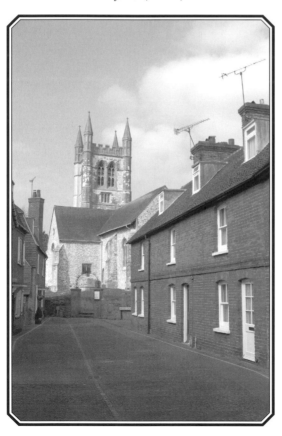

Farnham church has been the scene of many unexplained phenomena over the years. (Author)

outside the church have heard the singing of Latin chants coming from the body of an empty church and also a little old lady, who is seen to enter the church but never arrives inside. The church also has its own white lady who appears at the top of the tower and then jumps – to vanish, literally, in mid-air. I think this proves that Farnham can claim not only to be the most haunted town in Surrey but to also have the most haunted church.

GODALMING

My home town has a long history going back at least to the 7th century and this history is reflected in the numerous ghosts which now stalk the shadows of its narrow streets and ancient buildings. Many famous people have passed through this town, situated as it is about half way between England's premier naval station, Portsmouth, and the capital. Samuel Pepys, two Russian tsars and Admiral Nelson are just a few of the names which spring readily to mind. Then there were those many thousands of lesser mortals who rode, walked or crawled that route to fortune, adventure or death, which was for centuries the Portsmouth Road.

Tsar Peter the Great came here in 1698. He was en route to London and a boisterous stay at John Evelyn's house in Deptford. Peter had just come away from watching the English navy on manoeuvres and, with his mind buzzing with ideas to take back to Russia, he stopped with his entourage at the King's Arms in Godalming High Street. It was only a short stay but it has been claimed that the Russians spent the entire time in a riotous orgy of eating and drinking. So much did they consume that the landlord, James Moon, feared for his financial well-being, as they seemed uninterested in making any financial contribution. Obviously most of the young women of the town made themselves invisible or were whisked away by anxious fathers. When the Russian party left there was much relief amongst most Godhelmians, as the natives of the town are known. Following this, John Evelyn's beloved garden at his house, Sayes Court, was seriously vandalised during Peter's sojourn at Deptford. Russian sporting activities there included wheelbarrow racing, and such behaviour brought forth a succinct comment from the diarist's bailiff when he described the visitors as 'right nasty'. Evelyn stayed away and King William III eventually paid all the bills.

James Moon and the people of Godalming must have thought that they had seen or heard the last of such troubles, but they were wrong. Ever since then the King's Arms has been haunted by poltergeists and ghouls usually attributed to those Russian visitors of more than three hundred years ago. The most

The King's Arms at Godalming: do the ghosts of some of this ancient coaching inn's many famous visitors linger on? (Author)

common phenomenon is the noise from upstairs of raucous laughter and heavy footfalls. Then there is a series of loud 'clonks' as if someone has just thrown off their boots. These events may be related to reports of a strange figure dressed in old-fashioned clothes seen at an upstairs window. Downstairs in the bar over the years there have been many reports of items such as glasses of beer suddenly lifting up and dropping to the floor and packets of crisps being shaken out on the carpet by an unseen hand. Witnesses making such claims have been adamant that they were sober at the time. This reminded me of the old story of the publican who was asked about claims made by some of his customers that his establishment was haunted. 'The only spirits I've ever seen around here came out of optics' came the sardonic reply.

Brook House in Mint Street must be Godalming's most haunted building. It is said, though I have not managed to find any proof, that a previous owner hanged himself from an upstairs beam and that his ghost returns from time to time to the room where he killed himself. The unfortunate man has also been seen from across the street staring out of the window of the room. Dr Boyd who lived at Brook House for many years during the first half of the last century, also reported that he had seen the ghost of a Dr Mackenzie, who had once lived there. This was a friendly ghost who was probably just checking that the practice was still being run to the standards of his day.

Brook House also has a female ghost but, unlike Dr Mackenzie, she has terrified those who have seen her. The house is Georgian and, down the years, there were quite possibly many whose lives ended within its walls. This particular woman is thought to have died in one of the bedrooms from injuries received as a result of a fall down the stairs. A visitor staying at the house awoke one night at about 3 am and, as he was feeling rather thirsty, decided to make his way downstairs to the kitchen for a glass of water. As he entered the kitchen he saw standing by the table an old woman, but he quickly realised that he could see right through her. The kitchen was very cold and he felt very frightened. He beat a hasty retreat back upstairs to his bedroom without that glass of water. This same ghost has also been heard shuffling around the house

Brook House, Mint Street, Godalming, has one friendly ghost and another which is distinctly the opposite. (Author)

and slowly climbing the stairs to what was once the bedroom where she died. The house has been used as offices for some years and a friend of mine recently asked a woman, who was working in what had once been that bedroom, if she had ever seen a ghost. 'Strange things have happened here,' she replied mysteriously but, when pressed, refused to elaborate.

St Edmund's Roman Catholic church in Croft Road was built in 1906 and later St Edmund's Hall was opened further down the street. During the Second World War, the hall was used as a canteen for the many Canadian troops stationed in the area, especially those from Witley and Milford Camps. For many years after the war, the ethereal figure of a soldier regularly appeared in the hall, standing with a forlorn expression upon a face which witnesses found difficult to fix in their minds. This was thought to be the ghost of a Canadian soldier, who had no wish to return home to some unhappy situation at the end of the war, and this led him to commit suicide.

Church Street is the most attractive part of Godalming with numerous old houses, most of which are now shops. One of these, which is thought to date from the 15th century, was haunted for many years by the figure of an old man in Victorian dress. An old lady who lived next door was often disturbed at night by the sound of people running up and down the stairs, although all the shop staff had gone home. Several staff members also reported hearing strange noises and at least one of them saw the ghost in a 19th-century extension to the building. However, much of this ghostly activity seemed to have been focused around one particular member of staff and, when she left, the ghost went with her and has not been seen or heard since.

In 1869 the Reverend Kerry, curate of Puttenham, recorded an interesting incident at nearby Farncombe. In this story there is no apparent distinction between witch and ghoul, both of whom struck fear in the hearts of Victorian country folk.

'Pratt's father was returning one night from Farncombe to Compton. When he reached the top of the hill leading out of the village near the pound he fancied he heard something approaching,' wrote the curate. 'The sound grew more and more distinct but more and more unlike the progress of things material, scratch, scratch, scratch, footsteps none! One thing was certain the speed was terrific, so palpitating with fear he climbed the bank to be beyond the reach of danger. Scarcely had he done so, when to his horror he saw a hag withered and skinny taking her unholy course astride a hurdle. One look for Pratt sufficed. Off he bounded, not until he reached his cottage door did he dare to cast a glance behind him.'

Westbrook, on the outskirts of Godalming town, was the home of James Oglethorpe, who in 1732 sailed to America to found the colony, now state, of

Georgia. Various ghosts have been claimed for the house and it has been suggested that some of these hauntings relate to political intrigues at the time of the Jacobite Rebellion of 1745. Westbrook has certainly had some curious visitors. These include nine Indians and their chief, Tomochichi, from the Yamacraw tribe, who accompanied Oglethorpe to England when he returned in 1734.

Westbrook has been the Meath Home, now 'The Meath', a facility for epileptic women, since 1892, and its most well-attested ghost is that of a woman dressed in grey, who occasionally puts in an appearance. She turned up one night standing at the foot of the bed of a member of staff, who was not at all frightened as the ghost was considered to be 'a harbinger of good news'. A cynic might suggest that this explains why her visits are somewhat rare.

GUILDFORD

The ancient town of Guildford, famed for its steeply climbing High Street paved with granite setts, has been a stage for the work and play of diverse humanity ever since Saxons put the first log in the ground here, probably in the 7th century. There is much history to be found here amongst its venerable streets and narrow alleys, where the flicker of light and shade hints, perhaps, of the possibilities of a re-run of some scene from the past. The ordinary, the unusual, the mystifying and the macabre have all found a place in the history of the capital of Surrey.

Hideous screams are heard on a hill above the spot where King Alfred created a burgh or fortified Saxon settlement in the late 9th century. The town that grew up here soon became important enough to have a mint, where coins of several Saxon kings were struck. But in 1036 a terrible incident took place at Guildford, events which cannot fail to link the past to the present.

In that year Alfred, son of King Ethelred the Unready, and a claimant to the English throne, landed in England from Normandy. At Guildford Alfred and his followers were seized by Earl Godwin, who championed the claims of Harold, an illegitimate son of King Cnut. They were beaten and tortured and then nine men out of every ten were slaughtered. When sixty were left a further nine out of ten were killed leaving only six survivors.

Alfred had his eyes pulled out and was then taken to Ely were his suffering finally ended. The abbot of Jervaux, writing in the 12th century, described Alfred's death in graphic detail: 'indeed some say, that the beginning of his bowels being drawn out through an opening in his navel, and tied to a stake, he was driven in circles, with iron goads, till the latter parts of his entrails were extracted'. There was much indignation at such barbaric cruelty and a scribe recorded in the *Anglo-Saxon Chronicle* that, 'No more horrible deed was done in this land since the Danes came and peace was made. Now we must trust to the beloved God that they rejoice happily with Christ who were without guilt so miserably slain.' The murdered men appear to have been hastily buried on Guildown above the town, where their remains were discovered during the 1920s. It is here that, on a still night, the echoes of their anguished screams may be heard.

Soon after the Norman conquest in 1066, a castle was raised on a slope above the town to dominate and intimidate the local population into accepting their new masters. The castle achieved high status and, during the reign of Henry III, was developed into a royal palace. Much of the castle ruins survive, including the central keep or tower and Castle Arch. Other parts have been incorporated into later buildings, especially in Quarry Street. Most castles have a ghost or two but Guildford seems to be an exception. Apart from a brief occupation by the Dauphin of France in 1216, it played no part in major national events and has had, therefore, a rather more mundane history than most castles – but a castle without ghost stories does seem rather odd.

In medieval times, Guildford developed as an important commercial centre and market town, a role which it continues to fulfil to this day. By the 17th century the growth of Portsmouth as the nation's premier naval station brought many travellers through Guildford, and the town became well known for the hospitality of its inns, which lined the High Street. The White Lion, the Red Lion, the White Hart, the Swan and the Angel were all justly renowned throughout the land. The railway arrived in Guildford in 1845 and these famous inns quickly fell into decline. Now the White Lion is remembered in a shopping mall and the Swan in a lane linking the High Street with North Street.

Only the Angel Hotel survives. Its early 19th-century front hides a 17th-century fabric with a medieval vaulted basement or 'crypt' and, as might be expected, it has more than its fair share of ghosts. A presence and a sudden drop in temperature have been experienced by some visitors to the crypt, which once housed a restaurant, but it is upstairs, particularly in one of the bedrooms, that most of the hauntings have been recorded. There were incidents in 1969 and 1970, which were widely reported in the local press, in a bedroom named after the Prince Imperial of France, who stayed here with his entourage in the early 1870s. At about 8 o'clock one evening in November 1969, the receptionist answered a call from this bedroom but was met with silence. A woman who had earlier checked into this room was presumably responsible for the call but, despite prompting from the receptionist, she did

The reflection of a man dressed in military uniform was seen in a bedroom mirror at the Angel, Guildford. (Author)

not speak and the light on the switchboard remained on, indicating that the receiver had not been replaced. The staff member went to investigate and found the woman immobile and petrified with fear, claiming that she was strongly aware of a presence in the room.

A couple of months later a Mr and Mrs Dell booked into the same room. Mr Dell awoke at about 3 o'clock and could not get back to sleep. He decided to get up and sit in an armchair for a while. After a short time he stood up to go back to bed, glancing in the wardrobe mirror as he did so. He promptly fell back in the chair startled by the fact that he could clearly see the image of a man reflected in the mirror. But when he turned round to where the man should be, there was nothing there. Mrs Dell awoke, got out of bed and joined her husband in looking into the mirror. The image was there, a middle aged man with a dark moustache, dressed in military uniform, but when she turned around there was merely the scene of the undisturbed bedroom.

They watched the man for perhaps half an hour. The figure made no movement, dark eyes fixed and brooding under heavy eyebrows with the uniform looking foreign they thought. Mr Dell reached for a paper serviette and pen and made a sketch of the figure before it finally faded away. Had the man they had seen once been part of the Prince Imperial's entourage? There was no doubt that the Prince had stayed in the room, but there was also no evidence to link his visit specifically to the man whom Mr and Mrs Dell had seen. A mystery indeed, but one perhaps impossible to solve, as there have been no further reports of any unusual happenings in that particular bedroom.

The Angel is not the only haunted Guildford inn. The Plough in Park Street has a poltergeist thought to represent the spirit of a long-dead landlord who has returned to check that everything is in order. He tends to show his opinion on matters relating to the pub by unhooking a framed old photograph from the wall. The picture, showing the pub as it was over a hundred years ago, moves across the room and is then violently thrown down on the floor to land several feet from where it started. The ghost also opens and shuts doors and door handles are seen to move up and down.

In 2005 the landlord, Darren Walter, reported to the *Surrey Advertiser* that a friend staying on the top floor had 'heard someone walking up the stairs and closing a door behind them, when he knew we were all in bed'. He told the newspaper that the friend 'stayed for three months and although it freaked him out initially, he said he just got used to hearing it'. The ghost obviously likes music because on a number of occasions in the middle of the night the juke box has suddenly burst into life. The present landlord is pretty unconcerned about his spectral resident. 'This one seems quite friendly and I'd rather keep him unless he starts smashing anything else up,' he concluded.

On the opposite side of the High Street from the Angel is a branch of Waterstone's the booksellers, and it is here that there have been a number of unexplained incidents in recent years. In 1997 the remains of a medieval synagogue or a Jewish scroll reading room were found under the building, the discovery receiving a great deal of publicity at the time. Two hundred years ago the site was occupied by Guildford's prison. The noise of a heavy iron gate opening and closing has been heard followed by the sound of human gurgling. Voices have also been heard, bookshop staff have been tapped on the shoulder by an invisible hand, the lift has operated of its own accord, and the staff-room kettle has turned itself on. Also a friendly-looking old man has been seen on the stairs, only to disappear. 'It can almost certainly be ranked as a haunted house,' declared a local expert in the paranormal.

Guildford's old prison also extended into Quarry Street around the rear of the property on the corner of the junction with High Street. It is here that Waterstone's have their entrance for deliveries. The passer-by is greeted by a blank, faceless, impenetrable door more than vaguely reminiscent of the previous history of this part of the ancient street. Further down Quarry Street is another of the town's haunted pubs, the King's Head. It is claimed to be the most haunted building in Guildford and its ghosts include a old lady with a worrying stare, a skipping small child, plus a host of poltergeist activity. The old lady, grey and indistinct, was seen by a barman just as he called time. She is thought to be responsible for doors that suddenly fly open and she also causes the pub dog much consternation. He often barks frantically at the wall where a now blocked doorway once led down to the cellars.

Staff have often responded to a woman's voice calling up to them from the cellar, only to find the cellar empty. All sorts of strange things have been known to happen to electrical equipment in the pub. Workers repairing a ceiling found, for example, that their tools failed to work inside the pub but functioned perfectly when taken outside. A small girl clad in white has been seen several times at the pub's front door. Staff have nicknamed her Mary and her dress is thought to be Victorian. She skips through the bar and disappears through the French windows at the rear of the building.

Through much of its history, Guildford has not been without that ghastly spectacle of the public execution, which usually took place in the High Street. On 9th July 1709, one Christopher Slaughterford was hanged from gallows set up in front of the Three Tuns inn, a name still remembered in Tunsgate. Slaughterford had been found guilty of murdering his sweetheart, Jane Young, but to the end he protested his innocence. Not surprisingly he returned after the execution, a haunting that was described in a contemporary booklet or chap-book, as they were called. According to the writer he made a 'wonderful appearance to Joseph Lee his man, and one Roger Valler, at Guildford, in Surrey, on Sunday and Monday night last, in a sad and astonishing manner, in several dreadful and frightful shapes, with a rope about his neck, a flaming torch in one hand and a club in the other, crying vengeance, vengeance'. His reappearance occurred in a sandpit to the south-west of the town where the murder took place. Meanwhile, the jingling of his fetters was heard in the White Lion where he had been manacled, presumably in the cellar, to await his fate. It was also said that he appeared to several prisoners in Marshalsea prison, Southwark, where he had been held before being returned to Guildford for trial. This was clearly not good for business as far as the White Lion was concerned for the writer recorded that 'those who have heard the said unaccountable noise are afraid to go near the said place after daylight'. Marks and Spencer now occupy the site of the inn but, fortunately for them, the sound of Christopher Slaughterford's fetters has not been heard for many years.

Just a few doors down from Tunsgate, the shop at number 122 High Street was undergoing alterations in 1963, which seem to have disturbed the spirit of a limping woman. Her stumbling steps crossing the floor of the room above were heard on a number of nights by builders working late. The foreman described the ghost to a reporter from the *Surrey Advertiser*: 'All these sounds start at the same end of the room,' he related. 'The night after we took the doors out of the room above we heard the sound of a door swinging. Apart from the fact that the doors upstairs were non-existent, all the doors downstairs were wedged and were still wedged in the morning.' The workmen also heard voices which led them to believe that the ghost was a woman. They recalled that several times the faltering footsteps sounded as if they were climbing a flight of stairs but at that time the stairs had been removed. The limping woman whose steps 'echoed out from thin air' must have approved of the alterations to the shop as there has been no reference to her in recent years.

The almshouse in the High Street, known as Abbot's Hospital, is a very prominent building. It was built between 1619 and 1622 by order of George Abbot, who was born to a poor family in Guildford and rose to be Archbishop of Canterbury from 1611 to 1633. In one room above the gatehouse a man in 17th-century clothes appears, then fades. Courtly and composed, he has a resigned expression upon his face – a man who knows what the future holds for him perhaps.

It was here, in a room over the gatehouse, that the Duke of Monmouth was held overnight in July 1685 on his way to the scaffold. He was the illegitimate son of Charles II and had been banished abroad following his involvement in various plots to prevent his uncle, James, Duke of York, from becoming the next king. When Charles died in 1685, the Duke of York succeeded as King James II and, in June that year, Monmouth landed at Lyme in Dorset intent on seizing the throne. He gathered many West Country supporters opposed to the new Catholic king and they met James's army at Sedgemoor near Bridgwater in Somerset. However, from hopeful beginnings, the affair quickly turned to disaster as Monmouth's forces were scattered. Many were hunted down and killed or left to their fate at the 'Bloody Assizes' held by the infamous Judge Jeffreys at Dorchester. The gallows were certainly kept busy that summer. Monmouth himself was discovered cowering in a ditch disguised as a peasant and was brought to London for a special trial and then execution by the axe. It is said that it took five chops before his head was successfully severed from his body. But Monmouth still awaits his fate in that chamber at Abbot's Hospital where he spent one of his last nights on earth.

George Abbot was also responsible in 1629 for the building of a cloth hall at the rear of his almshouse on the corner of Jeffries Passage and what is now

The Duke of Monmouth stayed overnight in Abbot's Hospital, Guildford, en route to his trial and execution. (Author)

North Street. It was part of a scheme to revive the town's failing cloth industry, but it failed. The building then had a variety of uses over the centuries, including being used as a school until after the Second World War, but finally it was refitted as a shop and, in 1979, it became a branch of the Laura Ashley chain. During its conversion, workman were disturbed by an 'unfriendly spirit' and a painter and decorator working at night reported strange noises. 'We heard a sound like a trumpet. It came as a straight chord about every ten minutes. It was quite a regular sound,' he said. 'I would never work there on my own,' he continued, 'I wouldn't like to meet anything. I think if I had seen anything I would have died of fright. I made sure my mate was with me.'

Shop staff also became aware of various uncanny sounds and they also experienced a feeling that something or someone was watching them. In a stockroom on the top floor two young shop assistants were startled when they heard three loud, slow knocks on the window. They quickly ran down the stairs. 'We had to finish the stockroom but we felt someone was watching us,' said one of them. The stockroom always seemed to them to be unusually cold. One of the assistants also reported that in another room in the building, when working alone, she was disturbed by the sound of someone breathing behind her. There was no one else in the room. Early in the morning, before the shop opened, voices could be heard coming from an empty part of the building, and a cleaner also heard a small child singing. Several of the staff were agreed that there was something disturbing about the shop where each room had its own atmosphere. The Guildford branch of Laura Ashley moved a few years later to the main part of North Street.

In Upper High Street stands Guildford's ancient grammar school founded in 1509, although the present buildings fronting the street were constructed later in the 16th century. Near the school, an ethereal huntsman mounted on a grey horse comes riding by, soon to disappear. It has been suggested that he is a past pupil killed whilst chasing foxes.

Off York Road there was once a very large chalk pit which in 1969 was obscured by the construction of a multi-storey car park. Soon after the car park opened, two workman were concerned to see a lady wearing a long grey dress leaning over the parapet of the top storey. It was not long before their concern turned to fear when they realised that this was no living human being. They quickly fled the scene. Later, a Guildford housewife who had been brought up nearby related her experiences of this particular ghost. 'When I was a child I used to go and play in the chalk pit where the car park is and I used to talk to her. I never actually saw her but I used to feel she was with me and talking to me.' The housewife was convinced that the lady was a Quaker from the 18th century who had fallen in love with a non-Quaker. She was forbidden to marry

An ethereal huntsman rides by the Royal Grammar School, Guildford. (Author)

her man, ran off and was later found dead in the pit. Unfortunately, like so many of this sort of story, there are no facts surviving to support it.

'It sounds silly,' said the housewife, ' but there you are.' And 'there you are' indeed.

KINGSWOOD

There are curious stories that still circulate of murder and hauntings at the old vicarage at Kingswood in the Victorian period. St Andrew's church was consecrated in 1852 but the present vicarage nearby is of a later date. The original vicarage where the murder took place is situated some distance from the church and is now a private house.

It was June 1861 and the vicar, the Reverend Samuel Taylor, his wife and servants were away for a few days visiting family in Chertsey. Meanwhile, the parish clerk's wife, Martha Holliday, was employed to look after the house, especially during the hours of darkness. She slept there, alone. Then one night

At the Old Vicarage at Kingswood there is a tale of murder and haunting. (Author)

two burglars, who may have been aware of the vicar's absence, forced their way into the building, where they seized poor Martha Holliday and bound and gagged her. It appears that they were disturbed by a neighbour returning to the cottage next door because they departed in a hurry, leaving the poor woman trussed up. They stole nothing.

The following morning the parish clerk, anxious because his wife had not returned home to make his breakfast, went to the vicarage. He found the front door open and called for his wife. Getting no reply, he searched the house, finally making his way upstairs to the bedroom where his wife would have been sleeping. His terrible discovery there was reported in the *Sussex Express*. 'She was found dead in her night-dress on the floor of her bedroom ... her feet and hands tied by strong string.' One of the vicar's socks had been pushed firmly into her mouth, too firmly in fact. Martha Holliday had suffocated.

The hunt for the perpetrator of this terrible crime led police to a recently arrived German immigrant, whose birth certificate had been found rather conveniently dropped by the body. He was charged with murder but at the trial his defence were able to prove that he had been framed by two compatriots. Unfortunately, by then these two had made good their escape and the trail ran cold. The case had come to a dead end and it seemed likely that no one would ever be brought to trial for the murder of Martha Holliday. Some years later, however, events switched to Germany where two men stood accused of a murder in their homeland. It transpired that they were the same pair who had committed the Kingswood murder, and this time justice was about to catch up with them. They were found guilty by the German court and sentenced to death. A breakthrough for the Surrey Constabulary came shortly before their execution when the two confessed to the murder of Martha Holliday.

The Kingswood parish register records the burial of Martha Holliday, aged 55, on 15th June 1861 and that, you would think, should be the end of this intriguing incident. But a violent death sometimes results in the victim's unsettled spirit returning to the place where life was ended, and this was clearly the case at Kingswood. In 1876 the Reverend Taunton moved into the vicarage. It was not long before he became aware of a presence in the house and, in those peaceful moments of evening when alone, he would hear a rustling sound, which he likened to someone in a silk dress gently passing by his chair. However, Lillian, one of his daughters, was the most receptive of the family to the spirit's presence and on several occasions she actually saw 'a mysterious tall lady dressed in black'.

There were also strange happenings in the grounds of the vicarage and one particular event was carefully recorded in a letter written by another of the Reverend Taunton's daughters, Agatha, to a friend. She described how her sister, Lillian, had gone with a cousin to visit another sister, Alice, who was married to the vicar of nearby Headley. It was a Sunday afternoon and shortly before half past six the two young women returned to Kingswood. As they approached the vicarage, they saw, standing at the gate of the vicarage drive, a tall figure which, as they got nearer, began walking up the drive in front of them. It reached the house, then turned off and went round the side of the building and stopped by a large oak tree. Slowly, it turned round to face them and then started to come towards the two women, who were by now quite frightened. Lillian 'felt her hair stand on end and wished she could poke the figure to see if it was solid'. It walked with a 'queer loping step' and they saw that it was dressed in a long black garment with a white fringe at the bottom. On the top of its head was a shock of yellow hair but below that there was no face at all. It walked past, totally ignoring them and went through a small gate that led out of the gardens, and was gone.

Was this being anything to do with the death of the housekeeper many years before or did it represent something or someone else? It has been suggested that it was the ghost of a gardener, whose face was horribly mutilated as the result of an accident when he fell from a tree in the grounds.

I prefer to think that it was Martha taking a walk. The Reverend Taunton died in 1902 and his daughters went their various ways. Martha Holliday continued to haunt the place and some later occupants of the vicarage also saw that strange, faceless figure in the gardens. On two or three occasions the mysterious tall lady dressed in black was seen inside the house and other phenomena were also experienced, including locked and bolted doors that were found mysteriously open.

Houses were subsequently built in the grounds of the old vicarage and whether this brought an end to the activities surrounding the wandering spirit of Martha Holliday I do not know, but somehow I doubt it.

LINGFIELD

Probably the most famous haunting in the Lingfield area is that experienced at Puttenden Manor, a fine timber-framed yeoman's house of the

Puttenden Manor near Lingfield is haunted by two previous owners. (Surrey Archaelogical Society)

early 16th century. Records relating to Puttenden go back as far as 1164 and in 1477 it became the property of Reginald Sondes. It is thought that the Sondes family were responsible for the construction of the present house.

A house with so much history seems almost guaranteed to have a ghost or two and Puttenden does not disappoint. One owner of the house regularly experienced ghostly phenomena especially in the room used as a study and in two of the bedrooms. A curious aspect of the haunting relates to the re-creation of a variety of smells from the past, which happily include only pleasant odours. When the owner of the house smelt a whiff of perfume it was often accompanied with feeling a sensation akin to someone in a silk dress brushing past. At other times there was the smell of pipe tobacco despite the fact that no one in the house was smoking. Both these odorous ghosts are thought to be past owners of the house. Indeed, one source I consulted went as far as to say that the house was haunted by a Mr and Mrs Napier who bought the place in 1901 and have been reluctant to leave. The ghost of Mrs Napier has appeared in various places in the house, sometimes in company with a happy band of children. The same source also suggested a tale of jealousy within the Sondes family which led to murder but I have not managed to corroborate that particular twist in the fortunes of this ancient house.

Lingfield has another haunted house, Colboys in Hare Lane where, in the 1970s, two ethereal figures were reported. One was a male and the other female and the shadowy ghosts were seen both inside the house and in the gardens.

The Greyhound Inn at Lingfield is supposed to be haunted. In the past staff here have been upset when they have felt a peculiar sensation, as if they were being touched by an invisible presence. The landlord's dog also showed a marked dislike for the cellar. He refused to go anywhere near the stairs leading down below but stood at the entrance with hackles raised, growling and snarling, and stubbornly resisting any attempt to move him. The figure of a young boy has also been seen in the pub accompanied by a marked and sudden drop in room temperature.

LOSELEY HOUSE

Loseley, situated between Compton and Guildford, was built by Sir William More during the 16th century. Later, other members of the family made various additions to the building but today we see only part of the house. The west wing was demolished during the reign of William IV but Loseley remains a fine example of an Elizabethan mansion. The male line of the More family died out in the late 17th century and the Loseley heiress

The Tudor mansion at Loseley has more than a ghost or two.
(Author's Collection)

married Sir Thomas Molyneux. The estate is still owned by the More-Molyneux family.

In common with most ancient houses, Loseley has more than a ghost or two. In several rooms there is the feeling of being watched, and it is sometimes said to be 'not very pleasant'. A few years ago, an American staying in the house packed up and left in a hurry following 'a night of horror', although nothing tangible was seen.

However, at least two female ghosts glide about the house dressed in suitably old-fashioned clothing. The first is described as the brown lady, one presumes from the colour of her clothes, and gives out a happy feeling of peace to those who have caught sight of her. She is said to be associated with a painting discovered in the attic of the house in which she is depicted as an amiable woman with a gentle smile upon her face. In the 1970s she appeared to the lady of the house at the door to a bathroom. The second woman is a grey lady who is distinctly unpleasant, a murderess, who, in one account, killed her stepson so that her own son might inherit the house. In another version she is supposed to have killed her daughter by drowning her in the moat which once existed here. Now both the mother and her unfortunate victim float along the corridors of the house and into various rooms, the mother having a favoured bedroom. Maybe this lady has been somewhat maligned, for I have failed to find any historical evidence to support either of these supposed macabre events.

Loseley also has a mystery ghost, but those who have experienced it have refused to tell, and the whole matter seems veiled in secrecy. All very intriguing and definitely the sort of ghost story that I like best!

PUTTENHAM

The Reverend Francis Kerry was curate of the parish of Puttenham during the late 1860s. He was an inveterate collector of archaeological treasures and, when not tending to his flock, spent many hours scouring the countryside around the village for ancient pottery, prehistoric flint axes and the like. He also collected many fascinating details relating to lives and deaths, superstitions and beliefs, of his parishioners, which he carefully wrote up in a series of bulging notebooks.

On 15th November 1869 he recorded a weird incident under the heading 'Pharisees Exercising'. To the people of the more remote parts of west Surrey there existed small supernatural beings, who lived in a parallel world to humans somewhere between heaven and hell. The name Pharisees was a bible-influenced corruption of the dialect double plural 'fairieses', although these beings had little in common with the graceful winged spirits of poetry and prose. Sometimes the Pharisees would come into our world, more often than not to make mischief, to meddle and sometimes to strike fear.

'Old Master Durbridge worked at Shoelands,' wrote Reverend Kerry, 'between which and the village of Puttenham there is a hollow road lined with overhanging trees. The moon shone brightly, and the forked branches threw their entangled shadows on the ground, and the dark lines chased each other down his back as he journeyed on. 'Dark Lane' however had other travellers this evening besides Durbridge. Something was heard approaching, and through the chequered light he saw a sight which made his blood run cold. On they came, sweeping along, four weird riders, each astride a fold stake. Durbridge had barely time to throw himself into the hole where the water falls from the hop-garden, when like the wind the 'Pharisees' passed, the very leaves rising in circles behind them.'

Presumably the 'fold stake' referred to was a piece of wood used to support the hurdles of a sheepfold. Kerry added that 'the hole' was known as The Old Woman's Mop and was itself haunted by a headless old woman, who passed her time 'in the rainy season' washing her mop in the stream.

The lanes around Puttenham held many ghosts as Kerry's notes clearly

Dark Lane, Puttenham, where Old Master Durbridge's blood ran cold. (Author)

show. 'One dark night old John Fry and Joe Millbury on their way from Puttenham to Wanborough, saw lights rising and fading away over a certain spot in Wanbro' Lane, somewhere near the place where the lime kiln now stands. Singularly enough two skeletons were discovered there sometime afterwards, and one of the skulls was taken by a mischievous youth and placed on a gatepost at Flexford.'

In another entry in his notebooks, Kerry recorded an incident which perhaps illustrates best the very fine line that exists, if at all, between the folklore of the supernatural and the traditions of the ghost, ghoul and spectre. It must be added that the Pharisees have a particular attachment for horses and that many a Puttenham horse was 'borrowed' in the night for a devilish ride across the sky. 'Every 'Pharisee' has his favourite nag and will use no other. But the malignant night hag not only visits the horse in the stable, the carter in his bed is not secure from molestation. Richard Brown's brother, William, always sleeps with a Bible under his pillow, if however by any chance the Bible be mislaid, just as he is falling asleep he always hears the stealthy tread of the night mare coming up the stairs and in another second, he is groaning beneath the overpowering weight of his unwelcome visitor.' It is interesting to note how common are the incidents of sleepers awaking in the dead of night to feel the weight of 'something' at the end of the bed, a ghost or a Pharisee perhaps?

REIGATE

R eigate is an interesting town laid out in the lee of the ancient castle of the Earls of Surrey, with an old market house and a number of surviving ancient houses. But, now, the castle is just

A ghostly woman dressed in white has been seen outside Reigate church. (Author)

hummocks among gardens with a mock gatehouse built in 1771 and the roar of traffic below never ceasing. I remember Reigate so graphically as a child when visiting the town by car in the early 1950s. The sweep down Reigate Hill brought you to the entrance of a tunnel, where you plunged into the dark before, just as suddenly, emerging into the bright light in the heart of the town. Reigate has lost a certain sense of mystery since that road tunnel was closed to traffic.

The original settlement here was called Cherchefelle and was near to the parish church of St Mary, which now stands some distance from the present town centre. One evening in 1975, two women were walking past the church when suddenly there came the sound of a choir singing inside. Not unusual, you would think, just choir practice night, except it was not, for the church was empty, securely locked and in darkness at the time.

A few days later one of the women was walking along Chart Lane adjacent to the church when she saw someone making their way along the path to the church. As the woman drew nearer she could see that it was a lady of medium height wearing a white dress, possibly a wedding dress, but when she was only a few feet away from the her, she faded away.

There is a story retold by an anonymous chronicler in the 1820s that the ghost of a man was seen regularly 'in Judge Thurland's time ... at a stile as you go to Reigate Heath, which is now called Mad Meads Stile'. The chronicler wrote 'that the appearance of a man was frequently seen about this stile at night, and early in the morning, and that a labouring man who used to go to work early in the morning, and return after it was dark, frequently saw him'. The labourer mentioned what he had seen to several friends who advised him to try to speak to the wraith when next it appeared. So once more the labourer came to the stile and as before there was the apparition. He bravely asked the ghost why he haunted this spot. The ghost answered that 'he was murdered at that place, by a tinker who was then crying his trade at such town in Devonshire. That if they would seek for him they might take him ...'. The tinker obviously thought that he was safe so far away from where he had committed murder but he was found and they 'brought him to Reigate, before Judge Thurland .... He confessed the murder, was tried and condemned and hung on Reigate Heath.' Thereafter, of course, the ghost was never seen again.

A search of the records has shown that there was indeed a Judge Thurland who, in the 1660s, lived at a house called Great Doods and that he was a Justice at Reigate. But on the matter of murder and execution those records are mute.

RICHMOND

Until the reign of Henry VII, Richmond was known as Sheen. Its proximity to the river Thames, and being just a short boat trip upstream from London, made it a popular place with several monarchs, and Edward III built a palace here. Edward died at Sheen in 1377 but his successor, Richard II, demolished the palace, only for Henry V to rebuild it. Henry VII then rebuilt much of it yet again after a disastrous fire in 1499 and renamed it Richmond, after the North Yorkshire earldom he held. It was to Richmond that Elizabeth I came to die in 1603. She sat long hours in silence refusing to rest 'because she had a persuasion that if she once laid down she would never rise'. But lay down she finally did.

Little remains of the great Tudor palace at Richmond and the gatehouse is the only part to survive in its entirety. However, that is enough for a ghostly

The gatehouse of Richmond Palace, which is associated with the ghost of Queen Elizabeth I.
(Surrey Archaeological Society)

association with Elizabeth I to have become established. Her ghost was said to have been seen walking the galleries of the palace soon after she died. The palace was reduced to a ruin by the 17th century, and much of it was then pulled down, but Elizabeth still had the gatehouse where she was seen walking slowly or simply standing still. Perhaps she is re-enacting those last days of sleepless torment as she waited for death.

On the banks of the Thames hereabouts a handsome cavalier has been observed by a number of people at various times. 'He looked as if he had stepped out of a picture,' said one witness of this well-dressed ghost. 'We could see only his boots, his cloak and hat. The boots were peculiar, high and falling over the knee, his cloak large and round and thrown over his left shoulder in Spanish fashion, and his hat had a very wide drooping border and was so much on one side that we saw no face.'

'It became gradually transparent,' the witness reported as it came towards them, 'and we could see the bank and trees behind him. It got fainter and fainter, until it was gone.'

A little upriver from Richmond lies Ham House, a fine 17th century mansion with a long tradition of hauntings. Here stalks the tormented spirit of

A bust of the Duchess of Lauderdale who haunts Ham House near Richmond. (Surrey Archaeological Society)

the Duchess of Lauderdale. One source claims that the tap-tapping of her 'silver-headed ebony walking stick' can be heard as her ghost walks the 'dark corridors' of the house. This promiscuous lady, it is said, was once the mistress of Oliver Cromwell, but she married Sir Lyonel Tollemache. However, she murdered him at Ham in favour of a new husband, the Earl, later Duke, of Lauderdale.

The Duchess was the daughter of the first Earl of Dysart. She married Sir Lyonel in about 1647 and he died in 1669 but, for some time before his death, Elizabeth had been carrying on a relationship with Lauderdale. After the death of her first husband she had to wait a couple of years before her lover's wife passed away, but within six weeks Elizabeth and Lauderdale were husband and wife.

It is unclear when the suggestion arose that Elizabeth had murdered her first husband, but this is just the sort of tale of intrigue and murder which adds that extra spice to any ghost story. The Duchess had her critics, as she certainly enjoyed the good things in life but the imagination of the well-seasoned gossip knows no bounds. There is no doubt in some people's minds that her troubled ghost appears at Ham House. The origins of this story go back at least a hundred years and were retold by a certain Mr Hare according to Charles Harper in his book *Haunted Houses*. The story involved a small girl, the daughter of a butler at Ham House.

'In the small hours of the morning,' said Mr Hare, 'when dawn was making things clear, the child, waking up, saw a little old woman scratching with her fingers against the wall, close to the fireplace. She was not at all frightened at first, but sat up to look at her. The noise she made in doing this caused the old woman to look round, and she came to the foot of the bed and, grasping the rail with her hands, stared at the child long and fixedly. So horrible was her stare that the child was terrified, and screamed and hid her face under the clothes.' 'People who were in the passage ran in, and the child told what she had seen. The wall was examined where she had seen the figure scratching, and concealed in it were found papers which proved that in that room Elizabeth, Countess of Dysart, had murdered her husband to marry the Duke of Lauderdale.'

A good tale Mr Hare, but maybe a little unfair on the Duchess, I think.

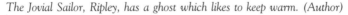

RIPLEY

ipley once sat astride the busy Portsmouth Road and has always had more than its fair share of pubs. For centuries travellers came by coach, horse or shanks's pony and stopped here to wash the dust from their throats. In those long hot summers before the First World War thousands of cyclists from London descended upon the village every weekend. Ripley has now been bypassed and is, perhaps, a quieter place these days.

The ghost at the Jovial Sailor is a strange individual to say the least because

The Jovial Sailor, Ripley, has a ghost which likes to keep warm. (Author)

it has shown a distinct dislike for the cold. It first appeared after renovation of the pub in 1978, when a fine inglenook fireplace was exposed from beneath later plaster and brickwork. A welcoming log fire on a chilly winter's day is a popular asset for any pub so the fireplace was fully restored. The customers certainly approved of the warming fire during the first really cold days of late November that year but so did the ghost. As the embers of the fire died away after closing time a shadowy figure wearing a cape was seen crouching by the fire trying to keep warm, but when approached it got up, made towards a lobby and vanished.

At the famous coaching inn, the Talbot, an ethereal figure, thought to be an old coachman, has been seen several times as a mere shadow descending a flight of stairs. The shadow then evaporates when it reaches the bottom step. In life this man, when stupefied with drink, fell headlong down the stairs and broke his neck. Now he returns to re-enact his sudden and tragic demise.

Between Ripley and Pyrford, the road traverses a myriad of water channels associated with the river Wey and the Wey Navigation. I remember a magnificent weather-boarded mill which stood astride one of the watercourses here until it was tragically burnt down in 1966. This is a tranquil spot, where

Although the monks at Newark Priory near Ripley were banished in 1538 they still exert a strange influence over the area. (Surrey Archaeological Society)

clear waters gurgle past the ruins of Newark Priory. The priory belonged to the Austin Canons and was founded in the late 12th century but the canons have long gone, thanks to King Henry VIII. Nearby is Homewood Farm, which is said to contain building materials and a staircase removed from the priory after the monks had been banished in 1538. But it was not just physical remains of the priory which found their way here, Homewood Farm is haunted, as a former occupant of the farm, Mrs Smith, recalled.

'While living there for a period of twenty years many unexplainable phenomena took place,' commented Mrs Smith. 'We were told the place was haunted when we moved in, but dismissed the idea. However, it wasn't long before the Black Canon made himself known. Often there would be the smell of toast burning' said Mrs Smith and she suggested, by way of an explanation, that the farm had once provided Newark Priory with bread. 'And shortly after one would hear a door bang or someone walking upstairs. Often the doors would open for no apparent reason and the dogs would watch 'nothing' pass through followed by another door opening.' Mrs Smith called the ghost Old Nick.

No one had actually seen the ghost until they had a visit from a man who claimed to possess psychic powers. 'You have a presence in the house', announced the man as he entered. 'I can see a man standing in this room with something over his head.'

'We had not mentioned ghosts, or whether it was male or female, and assumed he had seen Old Nick with his cowl over his head. Many times articles went missing only to turn up again days or weeks later where you left them, although one searched the house,' continued Mrs Smith. 'He was a friendly ghost and I think was guarding the priory belongings that had been built into the house.'

There can be no doubt that the canons of Newark Priory are a continuing influence on both residents and visitors to this ancient place. Their shadows are surely seen at dusk as the mist begins to rise above the green meadows and fields they once farmed.

SUTTON PLACE

Sutton Place, undoubtedly one of Surrey's finest houses, was built by Sir Richard Weston during the 1520s, a square house constructed in brick around a courtyard but now bereft of its north side, which was demolished in 1786. The part now lost included a magnificent Tudor gatehouse of four storeys with polygonal turrets, a very impressive way of

A Tudor lady wanders the corridors and rooms of Sutton Place.
(Author's Collection)

making your entrance that can still be appreciated today at Hampton Court. Sir Richard Weston was very successful in the dog-eat-dog court of King Henry VIII and many famous people came this way including the king himself. Weston was created a Knight of the Bath, a Gentleman of the Privy Chamber and rose to be Under-Treasurer of England. His popularity with the king did not, however, prevent Henry from ordering the beheading of Sir Richard's only son, who was implicated in the chicanery which brought down Anne Boleyn.

With such a history it is not surprising that Sutton Place is haunted. A Tudor lady stalks the long gallery as she has done so, apparently, for at least two hundred years. Some say she looks like Queen Elizabeth I. There is also a white lady, who has been seen and heard by both staff and visitors. She is thought to be the source of various very loud and violent crashing noises, which have been likened to the sound of furniture being smashed to pieces. The lady and her vandalism occur at night but by the morning any damage has been perfectly restored. Whether the nerves of those disturbed by her have also been restored is another matter.

THE TILLINGBOURNE VALLEY

My researches into the ghosts of Surrey soon took me along the beautiful little valley of the Tillingbourne, starting at Chilworth, in the west, not far from where the clear, sparkling waters of this rivulet pour into the river Wey. Benign and trout-filled, few could imagine the past history of this rippling stream, but at Chilworth there stood for almost three hundred years an important gunpowder works.

Here was dangerous work, which was kept well away from the houses of the hamlet. The workers wore special clothing without metal buttons and wooden clogs upon their feet. No chances were taken, for the slightest spark from toecap or stud could blow the works to kingdom come. Despite all the precautions, explosions, mostly fatal, occurred at regular intervals down the years and brought a succession of coroners and jurors to the Percy Arms in the village to view the body parts and conclude the cause.

Gunpowder production ceased at Chilworth in 1922 but parts of the works can still be traced today. It also left behind something less tangible as a reminder of the troubled and unsettling times at the Percy Arms. For years staff and customers experienced poltergeist activity at the pub. Doors slammed shut suddenly with great force and the night was disturbed by a noise like shovelling coal. Various vigorous rattling sounds and loud crashes surprised the staff but when they investigated nothing was found damaged and nothing moved. Meanwhile a bedroom at the pub had a reputation for disturbances and the feeling of a presence. Such activity was not confined to the period after closing time for in a busy bar objects would be thrown across the room, bar stools levitated and tankards smashed upon the floor. This was all witnessed by sober staff and maybe, sometimes, not so sober customers. Such events were considered to originate from the spirit of one of the unfortunate men who had perished in the Great Explosion of 1901, when six workers died and their remains were found scattered about this beautiful part of Surrey.

The church of St Martha looks down upon the green meadows of this now lovely place from its tree-clad eminence. In about 1977 a motorist was driving along White Lane nearby with a clear view of the church and hill. Imagine his surprise when he saw a house on the side of the hill where, to his knowledge, no house existed. 'I know Guildford quite well, and was astonished to notice a large white house situated halfway up the hill at St Martha's,' the driver told a *Surrey Advertiser* reporter. 'I stopped the car and got out to have a better look. It was definitely not the church itself, as I could see the silhouette of that to the right of the house at the top of the hill,' he continued. Later that evening he returned down the same route but of the house there was no sign. The

The view of St Martha's Hill from White Lane, where the mystery house was seen. (Author)

motorist later found out that a friend had similarly seen a house on the side of St Martha's Hill. 'He saw a building which he described as 'a wishy-washy outline of a white house' from almost the same spot in White Lane.'

The mystery house looked like a large white Georgian-style house illuminated from the outside. It also made its appearance to others. 'It was very large – almost a mansion,' recalled one witness. The origins of this house are unknown for no maps nor local documents make any reference to a house at that spot.

Next to Chilworth is the village of Albury, which has a somewhat curious history. The present village started life as the hamlet of Weston Street, with Albury itself lying half a mile or so to the east. However, ancient Albury became absorbed into the grounds of Albury Park in the early 19th century and the villagers were moved away. Now only the ancient Saxon church and one house, which was once the village inn, remain. The present Albury church was built in 1842 and Weston Street assumed the name of Albury.

The writer and poet Martin Tupper lived in Albury in the mid-19th century and much of the myth and legend of the area owes its origins to his fertile imagination. This is particularly true of the Silent Pool, where there are oft-repeated tales of the ghost of a 'fair maiden', who drowned in the pool in the days of bad King John.

The attractive village of Shere is next up the valley from Albury and nearby at Peaslake is Hound House. Parts of the present house date from the 16th century but it has been suggested that the site was once occupied by a hunting lodge used by King John in the pursuit of his sport. It is said that some of the king's hounds were kennelled here. Personally, I think that much of John's reputation has suffered from a bad press but evil royalty and nobility always seem to generate a ghost or two.

Hound House is a fairly recent renaming of 'Greets' or 'Gritts' and it is haunted by a pack of dogs. On silent paws they lope across the garden to the back of the house, leap through one of the windows, regardless of whether it is open or closed, and vanish just as silently as they came. Perhaps the source is just a little more prosaic and relates to the Reverend Samuel Godshall, who lived at Albury in the 18th century, and is definitely known to have kept hounds here. Hound House also has a friendly male ghost. He divides his time between sitting around relaxing in the kitchen or visiting the former servants' quarters but he strikes no fear in the hearts of those who see him, rather the opposite.

The ghosts at Hound House, Peaslake, include a silent pack of hounds. (Author)

The Tillingbourne Valley has many ponds made by the damming of the stream to provide the water to drive the numerous mills for flour, gunpowder and paper which once stood hereabouts. At Abinger Hammer the name is a reminder that there were water-powered hammers here which were used in iron making, a once important industry in these parts. Associated with the ponds comes the story of a lost coach last seen sinking into the unplumbed depths, amidst the screams of passengers and coachmen, the snorts and whinnies of the maddened steeds. On sombre nights when the wind blows chill these sudden deaths are re-enacted. The pounding hooves and anxious shouts precede an ear-splitting crash. A wailing moan comes clear across the water, then silence.

From Abinger Hammer it is just a short drive along the road to Wotton. There is not much to see in terms of village, one or two cottages, a pub and, glimpsed tantalizingly through the trees, the medieval church of St John. The pub is known as the Wotton Hatch but I believe it used to be called the Evelyn Arms after the local landowning family who lived nearby at Wotton House. Their fortune was based on the monopoly to manufacture gunpowder granted

Wotton House has a number of ghosts. (Surrey Archaeological Society)

by Elizabeth I and their most famous family member was John Evelyn, the diarist and gardener, who was born at Wotton in 1620.

Wotton House still stands, although much altered since John Evelyn's day but his garden is still substantially intact. Until about 20 years ago the property was leased to the Home Office and used as a staff college for the Fire Service. During that time there were a number of reports of ghostly manifestations. Poltergeist activity included small objects being moved and then turning up in unlikely places and sash windows opening and shutting of their own accord. Some parts of the house were inexplicably cold, even on hot days. Door handles moved when the room beyond was known to be empty and in some rooms both staff and students reported a presence, coupled with a feeling of stress and anxiety. However, it was the night porters who had most to say on the matter of ghosts.

In the early hours of 2nd April 1964, when Mr A H Welch was on duty in the entrance hall, he heard the front door quietly open and close. He looked up to see a very short man walking across the hall to a table set on the left side of the hall fireplace. It was a bitter cold night but there was no heating in the hall. The time by the night porter's watch was five to three. 'He paused to look at something on the table, or so it seemed,' said Mr Welch. 'He was very short, say four feet or less. He was wearing a hairy brown tweed jacket and darker trousers, and was carrying something long under his left arm, which I 'knew' to be fishing tackle. He had very little white or grey hair and long Dickensian whiskers, rather sparse, white, and swept out sideways,' continued Mr. Welch. 'I had the impression of tranquillity and a kindly face. He was unhurried, but perhaps a little fussily engaged on whatever he was about, and the pause by the table wasted a moment or two. As he moved towards the door he just wasn't there anymore.'

During the time that the man was at the table the night porter asked him if he could help. 'He did not answer, and never gave any sign that he knew I was there. He never looked in my direction,' said Mr Welch. 'I did not have the 'cold' sensation and was not the least alarmed. I wondered later if his shortness could be accounted for by an old floor level lower than the present floor.'

One night another porter heard the sound of footsteps crunching on the gravel outside approaching the front door. He was expecting the late return of a staff member. The porter got up and went to the door to open it but, when he did so, there was no one there. Then a chill wind got up and something invisible pushed past him. Later the porter heard further footsteps and, looking up, he saw the hazy shadow of a man. The footsteps ceased but the shadow made its silent way across the hall heading towards the corridor, only to disappear.

Bishop Samuel Wilberforce 'appeared' at Wotton House shortly after his death. (Surrey Archaeological Society)

Wotton House was also the scene of a curious incident in 1873 relating to the sudden death of Samuel Wilberforce, the Bishop of Winchester. The bishop and a companion were riding nearby through Deerleap Wood on their way to Holmbury, when the bishop happened to remark that he had never visited Wotton House. He was a biographer of Lady Godolphin, and mentioned that he would particularly like to visit the Evelyn family home as it housed a portrait of the said lady. Shortly after making this remark Wilberforce's horse stumbled and the bishop was thrown heavily and killed. At that moment, William Evelyn, his brother, and two friends were sitting in the dining room at Wotton House when they heard a noise at the window. Imagine their surprise when they looked up and saw the face of Samuel Wilberforce peering in. Evelyn had met the bishop on several occasions elsewhere, but was perplexed that he should make such a visit unannounced. The group waited for the butler to bring news of the bishop's arrival but nothing happened. They went outside and searched the gardens but the bishop was nowhere to be seen. It was sometime later that news of Samuel Wilberforce's death reached Wotton House.

WAVERLEY

In 1128 a group of Cistercian monks made the long and sometimes perilous journey across the English Channel from Normandy to a beautiful and serene spot on the banks of the river Wey near Tilford. It was the Bishop of Winchester, William Giffard, who brought these monks to this tranquil place, where the northern branch of the river flows through a narrow verdant valley.

They were the founding fathers of Waverley Abbey, the first Cistercian monastery in England.

The Cistercian Order was founded by an Englishman, Stephen Harding, and took its name from its chief abbey at Citeaux in Burgundy. The monks were clad in white in contrast to the more 'worldly' Benedictine monks, the Black Monks. The rules which marked out the daily lives of the White Monks were severe. One rule stated that 'none of our houses are to be built in cities, in castles, or villages, but in places remote from the conversation of men'. In Surrey they had found their perfect place. By the end of the 13th century, Waverley had developed from small beginnings into an architecturally magnificent range of buildings with estates and influence over many miles of the surrounding countryside. All this was, of course, swept away when Henry VIII dissolved the monastery in 1536.

Even today this is a calm, spiritual place. The crystal waters of the Wey gurgle happily past the few abbey ruins that remain. But here and there a pillbox or a tank trap are reminders of more recent history. All leave a strong mark upon the psyche.

Across the meadows from the ruins is Waverley Abbey House, which was used as a military hospital during the First World War. In 1925 that

The ruins of the Cistercian monastery of Waverley were haunted by the restless spirit of Peter de Rupibus, Bishop of Winchester. (Author)

indefatigable collector of ghosts stories, Lord Halifax, received a letter from Mrs Anderson, the owner of the house and abbey ruins.

'Mrs Dundas [Lord Halifax's sister] left us this morning,' Mrs Anderson wrote. 'She has been staying with us for the last week and made me promise to write you the following little story of what occurred here during the war, when our little house was turned into a hospital for wounded men.' Mrs Anderson then went on to relate that a sitting-room in the house was turned into a chapel for the Roman Catholic patients. The services there were led by Father Robo, a well-known figure in Farnham who wrote several works on the history of the town. 'One Easter he told me that he wanted to have High Mass in my little sitting-room. He had obtained permission for the service from the Pope, in recognition of what we had done for the Roman Catholic wounded. It had always been supposed that the Abbey was haunted by the ghost of a cardinal, whom some declared they had seen walking about the place.'

Lord Halifax deduced that the spectre was unlikely to be a cardinal but was possibly Peter de Rupibus, who was also known as Peter des Roches, who became Bishop of Winchester in 1205 and died in 1238. Peter's heart and bowels were buried in Waverley Abbey church and the rest of his body in Winchester Cathedral. In 1731, his heart was reportedly found at Waverley contained within two lead dishes that had been soldered together. Sadly, this interesting relic has been lost. Mrs Anderson thought that he continued to walk the Abbey ruins and her house because the living were no longer praying for his soul. A figure dressed in 'cardinal's robes' appeared frequently to both patients and nurses in the large drawing-room, where a ward of 18 beds had been set up. Sometimes it was seen by several people at the same time. 'The general belief was that the abbey was under a curse, as having been the property of the Church and stolen from her,' claimed Mrs Anderson.

The High Mass was duly celebrated on Easter morning, when the priest conveyed a message from the Pope that the curse on Waverley Abbey had been removed by His Holiness.

'We were to pray for the cardinal, which thereupon we did, after which his soul would rest in peace. This happened 7 or 8 years ago, and since that day the cardinal has not been seen again,' wrote Mrs Anderson. Her comments would appear to date the Easter mass to 1917 or 1918.

All sorts of unsubstantiated myths have grown up around this well-documented ghost. Some have suggested that he is still 'drifting around' and 'guarding a horde of hidden treasure'. Another source has a monk who committed some deed so foul that he was hanged, drawn and quartered and now walks the ruins of Waverley looking for his entrails. I think I prefer Lord Halifax's version of events.

WEST HORSLEY

A vast array of the famous and the infamous have connections with the county of Surrey, and the village of West Horsley itself can claim quite a few. Enter that celebrated Elizabethan, Sir Walter Raleigh, the first importer, so it is said, of tobacco and the potato, who is perhaps only overshadowed by Frances Drake amongst our early seafaring heroes.

Sir Walter's story touches both West Horsley and Beddington and in both places it is more than slightly bizarre. His exploits made him popular with Elizabeth I, who knighted him in 1585, but he fell out of favour in 1592 when it was revealed that he was carrying on with one of the queen's ladies-in-waiting. He later married the lady but such over-confidence put Sir Walter in the Tower for the first of his three visits to that establishment.

During the reign of the queen's successor, James I, Raleigh fell completely from grace and spent twelve years in the place. He was released for a final unsuccessful trip to South America, only to be shoved back in again upon his return. By 1618, James had had enough of the man and poor Sir Walter was beheaded. Meanwhile, Sir Walter's son, Carew Raleigh, had purchased West Horsley Place, where he lived with his mother until she died in 1647.

Following his execution, Sir Walter's body was duly buried, but his head did not accompany the body to his grave. It was exhibited on a spike before being rescued and given to his widow. She had the head embalmed and kept it for 29 years in a bag on a shelf in West Horsley Place. It is said that when she died this grisly memento was passed to Carew Raleigh and eventually it went with the son to his grave in West Horsley church. Apparently, when the grave was reopened in 1703 it did, indeed, contain two heads. The Raleighs were connected to the Carew family, who were the squires of Beddington, and some say, that for this reason,

The driveway of West Horsley Place, where the ghost of Lady Raleigh has appeared, clutching a leather bag. (Author)

the body was interred in the churchyard at Beddington. There its shade makes an occasional appearance searching for its head.

Over the years there have been a number of reports of a strange-looking woman seen either outside West Horsley church on the Guildford Road or at the entrance to the driveway of West Horsley Place. The figure is 'pale and wispy' and she is wearing a long habit, variously described. However, one quite distinctive factor is common to all these reports, the woman carries an unusual style of round leather bag, a bag big enough to take a human head.

WEYBRIDGE

Brooklands motor-racing circuit was built just south of Weybridge and opened in 1907. It was the world's first purpose-built track, an imposing modern structure with bridges and dramatically curved concrete banking. Not long after it opened it also became a pioneering centre in the development of aviation. Indeed, much transport history was made at Brooklands, where vast crowds came to be enthralled by a spectacle where sudden death beckoned just beyond a split second's miscalculation.

Brooklands closed at the outbreak of war in 1939, never to reopen for motor-racing. For many years it was a major centre of aircraft production. But the spirit of the early days of motor-racing lingered on and perhaps its ghosts also remained to re-live the good and bad times, when emotions and excitement ran high.

The Brooklands Society was founded to preserve the history of the place with the aim of opening a museum on site. The Society proved to be spectacularly successful in its aim and now there is one of England's most exciting museums at Brooklands. However, in the 1970s there was still a great deal of work that needed to be done before hopes could become reality. The clubhouse and some of the track had survived, and society members laboured for thousands of hours to clear sections of it. Whilst involved in this work, some of them became aware that more survived of Brooklands than just its physical remains. Strange phenomena were reported, particularly from the area near to Members' Bridge. In 1975 John Wall, a society committee member, reported to the *Weybridge Review* that he was determined to find out the reason for these 'strangest of sensations'.

'Just after Easter a crowd of us drove out to the banking near the bridge,' he told a reporter, 'and, although we'd all previously scoffed at the idea of ghosts as such, we took with us a gentleman who was known to experience psychic phenomena.' The psychic claimed that the area near the bridge was haunted

A surviving section of banking of Brooklands racetrack, where a number of ghostly manifestations have been reported. (Author)

and he made a sketch of what he had seen. 'The shock came when we saw the sketches,' exclaimed John Wall, 'for several of us recognised two portraits, one of whom was Donovan, an original Brooklands mechanic.'

'There's definitely something up there, whatever it is,' said a previously sceptical fellow committee member. Security man, Tom Balchin, related a frightening experience which he had one night as he stood outside the old clubhouse and looked across to a steep incline known as Test Hill. Suddenly, quite clearly, he saw a 'gigantic blob of black'. 'There was a sound of crashing, splintering metal or wood up on Test Hill and I was petrified to the extent that I could not move,' he reported. 'Test Hill was still overgrown at that time, but two days later when I plucked up courage to investigate, not a blade of grass, not a branch of a tree had been broken,' he exclaimed. 'There is definitely something strange in that area, and I'm a level-headed chap who doesn't imagine things.'

Some of these hauntings have been linked to the death of Percy Lambert at Members' Bridge in 1913, whilst he was attempting to break a world speed record. The ghosts near Test Hill may have something to do with a mechanic,

Ted Allery, who 'died in a most horrifying crash', which also killed a spectator as well as injuring several others.

'An optical illusion, an acoustic freak? Well, we can't all be wrong, so there must be something that gives rise to this eerie sensation on Test Hill, Members' Bridge and the banking up there,' concluded John Wall.

WIMBLEDON

There is more to Wimbledon than two weeks of lawn tennis and a football club that has now decanted to Milton Keynes. Yes, a new club has arisen as if by magic, and there are ghosts aplenty here as I discovered when I was kindly given a copy of *Mysterious Wimbledon* by the book's authors, Ruth Murphy and Clive Whichelow.

Many famous people have had connections with Wimbledon over the years including the inventor of radio, Guglielmo Marconi. This genius of a man was a regular visitor to Gothic Lodge, the home of Sir William Preece, chief engineer at the Post office. During one visit Marconi set up a transmitter in Sir William's garden and sent radio messages to the Post Office headquarters in London. But Marconi was also interested in another form of radio waves, those which carried messages from the dead. He believed that there was an electrical force present throughout the universe and that it carried the complete record of life. He was not the only one to conclude that the past continued to exist in a different plane, but he was convinced that it was possible to build a machine through which contact could be made with the departed. Who is to say that Marconi was wrong? Unfortunately, he died in 1937 still seeking to perfect his machine.

Wimbledon Theatre is haunted by a witch-like ghoul. (Author)

Since his death research has continued into what has become known as electronic voice phenomenon, or EVP for short. There have been many incidents where electrical equipment such as recording machines and telephones has picked up what are thought to be sounds emanating from beyond the grave. That research has so far failed to come up with any logical explanation.

Since it opened in 1910, Wimbledon Theatre has seen a long succession of the famous in the arts and entertainment come to tread its boards. Few theatres seem to be without a ghost or two and here is no exception. In 1980 the manageress, who lived in a flat above the theatre, was confronted in her bedroom by a hideous-looking grey lady whose only visible parts consisted of a head and torso. A terrifying spectre, with all the other useful parts of her body completely missing. This segmented ghoul proceeded to utter a witch-like cackle as it disappeared through the ceiling.

Several visitors to the theatre have felt a presence and this has been put down to the grey lady. She has made appearances in various parts of the theatre including the front row of the gallery and even, apparently, the ladies' toilet. She has also been blamed for several poltergeist-like activities such as the turning on of taps in the middle of the night and various malfunctions of the sprinkler system. On one occasion, when the system was set off for no apparent reason, staff had to lower the safety curtain in a hurry in an attempt to stop the orchestra pit from being flooded. The attempt failed but, even with the pit awash, it was found afterwards that the safety curtain itself had remained totally dry.

Wimbledon Theatre also has a male ghost who haunts one of the boxes. He is well-dressed and has been identified as John Mulholland, the man who founded the theatre and died in 1925.

It is curious how a particular street or road can become the focus of ghostly activity. In Wimbledon's case the road is Hillside. The explanation probably lies in the fact that at one time there was a concentration of psychically-sensitive people who regularly visited one of the houses here. From 1934 until 1941, a spiritualist group was based in a house which became known as 'The House of Red Cloud'. The leader of the group was a then famous medium, Estelle Roberts, whose spirit guide was claimed to be an American Indian called Red Cloud.

Over the years Estelle Roberts had many famous adherents including the politicians, Ernest Bevan and George Lansbury, and King George II of Greece. Sir Arthur Conan Doyle, an active spiritualist for many years and one-time resident of Surrey, also knew Estelle Roberts well. However, he died in 1932 before she came to Wimbledon. The House of Red Cloud became famous throughout the country as many spiritualist events were organised from here, some involving national newspapers such as the *Daily Sketch* and *Sunday Pictorial*. When Estelle Roberts moved away in 1941, spiritualist activity came to an end.

However, the spirits did not leave Hillside, and there have been a number of incidents here since then. One resident couple have seen the ghost of a young girl on two occasions in their garden. She was described as 'aged about twelve', wearing 'a light close-fitting chemise style garment'. The girl appeared late in the evening between 11 and 12 o'clock – once in the summer and again on a cold frosty night in January. She was seen walking towards the house but she then turned away and disappeared. Poltergeist activity was experienced by the couple inside the house with various items suddenly being moved, such as a fork which flew off the table when nobody was around. In another incident, ink stains appeared on a wall and ceiling although there was no ink in the house, but the stains had strangely vanished before the house's owner had a chance to clean them off.

The occupants of another house in Hillside experienced a very weird phenomenon relating to an upstairs room. At times they found that, once inside the room with the door shut, it was impossible to get out again. Those outside had no trouble opening the door but from the inside it would not budge. It seemed to be held by an invisible force. A woman was alone in the house one night when she found herself trapped in the room, and she became increasingly aware that she was sharing it with some form of 'malevolent spirit'. So terrified did she become that she climbed out of the window to escape. The story certainly sounds like the stuff of some of our worst nightmares!

WOKING

The origins of the new town of Woking are unique. Firstly, in 1838 came a railway station set down in the middle of the barren, almost uninhabited, Woking Common. Next came the sale of the common in 1852 to be developed as a huge cemetery to accommodate the dead of the rapidly-expanding metropolis of London. The establishment of the cemetery was the work of the grandly named London Necropolis and National Mausoleum Company, who also sold off some areas of the common for building development. Thus the present town of Woking and the Brookwood Cemetery came into being.

The burial of our Victorian ancestors in the cemetery was carried out in a well-ordered and efficient manner, although I hesitate to suggest that it was

The 'Ghost Train' arriving at Brookwood Cemetery. (Surrey History Centre)

mass-production burial. Specially-designed trains carrying coffins and mourners departed according to the timetable from the company's own platform at Waterloo Station. A branch off the mainline at Brookwood then brought the train right into the cemetery, where there were individual stations for the different religious denominations. It was not long before this railway service from London became known as 'the ghost train'. On arrival, the mourners were amply catered for with a refreshment room serving tea, coffee and mineral waters. Alcoholic drinks were also served and it is said that a sign above the door proudly proclaimed 'spirits served here'.

Whatever spirits there might be at Brookwood, there is undeniably that feeling of a presence which can be experienced in any place where the dead lie. But from the town of Woking and its suburbs have come many reports of ghostly manifestations. At a house in Heathside Road there have been several reports over the years of strange sounds from an empty bedroom. Slow footfalls, muttering and murmuring, crying and moaning, followed by shrieks and screams that could curdle the blood, have brought terror to occupants of this unfortunate place. At one point, the noises reached such a crescendo that the police were called by passers-by who thought that there was a murder taking place in the house.

The *Woking News and Mail* reported that the origins of these hauntings go

From an empty house in Heathside Road came blood-curdling screams. (Author)

back to 1904, when two sisters, described as middle-aged, moved into the house. One of the sisters gradually went insane while the other sister tried to cover up the fact by hiding her away in the house. She kept her locked in an upstairs bedroom and it was not until the woman died in 1936 that the truth of her imprisonment became known. Since then her ghost has continued to pace up and down the room in which she was held captive, her howls of insanity sometimes shattering the stillness of the night.

The original Saxon settlement of Woking can be found about two miles away on the banks of the river Wey. Nearby are the scant remains of a once important royal palace which was popular with both Henry VII and his son, Henry VIII. I have no reports that the site itself is haunted but, on a still, cold night an ethereal mist can be seen floating across this place carrying, maybe, just a hint of possibilities.

In the Old Woking Road there have been several incidents when passing motorists have been startled by a monk-like form clad in a long, dark habit, which has suddenly appeared from the blank side-wall of a house. It crosses the road and then vanishes. When a motorcyclist came upon the monk, he promptly fell off his machine in fright and the unlucky man ended up in hospital. This figure has been associated by some with the Austin Canons of Newark Priory situated just over a mile away.

There is a report of a haunted house in the High Street, Old Woking, but the ghost here is felt rather than seen. One night it 'appeared' to the couple living there as they lay in bed reading. They sensed something crossing the bedroom that brushed past their bed and then 'disappeared' through the wall. The couple's cat was disturbed by this unseen visitor, spitting and clawing at thin air in its fright. The couple also heard unaccountable noises and doors in the house opening and closing without human or animal assistance.

In 1932, a retired vicar, the Reverend Thomas Outram Marshall, arrived at St Paul's church, Maybury, dressed ready to help at the service of Holy

Communion being conducted by a visiting prebendary, the Reverend Wilson Carlile. Enquiries later revealed that the Reverend Marshall, who lived nearby in Oriental Road, had died just an hour or two before the service started.

In 1900, Edwin Lutyens, one of Britain's most famous architects, designed a house for Gerald Balfour, the brother of Lord Arthur Balfour. The house on Hook Heath, south west of Woking town centre, was completed in 1901 and named Fishers Hill. It is said that Arthur, who became Prime Minister from 1902 to 1905, got his first job in the Cabinet courtesy of his Uncle Robert, Lord Salisbury, who was Prime Minister at the time. It is suggested that the new appointee owed his job solely to his family connection, giving rise to the expression 'Bob's your uncle'. In international politics Arthur Balfour is best remembered as the politician who, in 1917, made the written declaration of British government support for 'the establishment in Palestine of a national home for the Jewish people'. This became known as the Balfour Declaration.

As a young man Arthur Balfour had fallen in love with Mary Littelton but the romance ended tragically when she died suddenly in 1875. Balfour was devastated and he was to remain true to the memory of his lost love for the rest of his life. He never married. Both Arthur, Gerald and their sister, Nora Sidgwick, the first principal of Newnham College, were much involved in psychical research and the two brothers also had terms as presidents of the Society for Psychical Research. It was natural that with Arthur's strong feelings for Mary, he would try to communicate with her via a medium.

Mrs Coombe-Tennant, a friend of the Balfours, and a well-known medium who operated under the pseudonym of Mrs Willett, agreed to lead a series of séances where attempts were made to contact the dead woman. Some of these sessions took place at Fishers Hill, and were reported as 'a remarkable series of communications' and it is said that a vision of Mary Littelton appeared at one point. It is interesting to speculate on what our 21st-century media would have made of such revelations that a leading politician was involved in psychical research. Arthur Balfour died at Fishers Hill in 1930.

Imagine the railway at Woking in the days when steam ruled the line. An express, perhaps the 'Bournemouth Belle', is pounding down the line, all smoke, steam, demonic power, the cab lit up with the red-hot glow of the firebox as the fireman piles on the coals. For a brief instant the driver spots a man, bearded and wearing old-fashioned clothes, lurching unsteadily across the rails right into the path of the train. Is he deaf, this hapless figure, a man oblivious to the threat, who is quickly sent to oblivion under the scything, unrelenting wheels? The gruesome deed is done and the incident reported. But a search finds nothing, no scrap of clothing, blood or bone, the man has simply disappeared.

The line near Woking is haunted by a long-dead railway worker, who perished beneath the wheels of a passing train. (Author)

This macabre event was re-enacted several times down the years but no grisly remains were ever found. Sometimes screams, coupled with the frantic sound of an engine's whistle, were heard at a time when there was nothing and no one on the track. All these incidents were thought to be connected with a tragedy that occurred at Woking during the Victorian period. A gang of platelayers were at work on the line late one night. For their safety they relied upon the lookout man to warn of approaching trains, but on that particular night this man was drunk and he fell asleep on the job. As a train bore down upon the men, no warning shout was heard as, heads down, they worked on in the gloom. The entire gang died, as did their slumbering lookout, who now walks the line, trapped in that limbo between heaven and hell, searching for his lost companions.

· Bibliography ·

Alexander, Matthew, *More Surrey Tales*, 1986.

Chouler, W H, *Tales of Old Surrey*, c.1978.

Coxe, A D Hippisley, *Haunted Britain*, 1973.

Cluett, D *et al*, *Croydon Airport: The Great Days 1928-1939*, 1980.

Dictionary of National Biography.

Forman, Joan, *The Haunted South*, 1978.

Fortescue, S E D, *People & Places, Great & Little Bookham*, 1978.

Green, A, *Our Haunted Kingdom*, 1974.

Halifax, Lord, *Further Stories From Lord Halifax's Ghost Book*, 1937

Harper, Charles G, *Haunted Houses*, Revised Edition, 1924.

Holland, Coffey, *Dorking People*, 1984.

Horsley Countryside Preservation Society, *Around and About Horsley*, No.109, Winter 1984/85.

Janaway, John, *Ghosts of Surrey*, 1991.

Janaway, John, *Surrey: A County History*, 1994.

Janaway, John and Mirylees, Duncan, *Some Surrey Spooks and Spectres*, c.1983.

Lane, Michael, *Surrey Lore and Legend*, 1999.

Larcombe, Nancy, *Captain White's River Life*, 1985.

Malden, H E, *The Victoria History of the County of Surrey*, 4 Vols, 1902.

Mitchell, Frances J, *The Manor House, Byfleet*, Surrey Archaeological Collections 20, 1907.

Murphy, Ruth and Whichelow, Clive, *Mysterious Wimbledon*, 1994.

Nairn, Ian and Pevsner, Nikolaus, *The Buildings of England: Surrey*, 2nd Ed. 1971.

Newspapers Various, *Surrey Advertiser, Surrey Mirror, Surrey Comet, Sussex Express*.

Parrett, Jean, *Haunted Farnham*, 1993.

Stewart, Frances D, *Around Haunted Croydon*, 1989.

Stewart, Frances D, *Surrey Ghosts Old and New*, 1990.

Taylor, David C, *Cobham Characters*, 1997.

Vulliamy, C E, *The Onslow Family*, 1953.

Willis, S Cloudesley, *A Short History of Ewell and Nonsuch*, 1948.

Spence, Jeoffry, *Caterham Court and its Legends*. Bourne Society Local History Records, Book III, 1964.

Weybridge Review, 30th July 1975.

·Index·